D0578202

Just come and visit Rocky Ridge
Please grant us our request,
We'll give you all a jolly time—
Welcome the coming; speed the parting guest.
—LAURA INGALLS WILDER

In remembrance of Roger Lea MacBride and Connie Tidwell, who were instrumental in helping to share this cookbook with the readers of the Little House books.

The publisher extends thanks to the following people for their assistance in the making of this book: Jean Coday and the staff of the Laura Ingalls Wilder–Rose Wilder Lane Home and Museum, and Neta V. Seal. The original cookbook is part of the large collection of artifacts preserved at Laura Ingalls Wilder's longtime home, Rocky Ridge Farm, in Mansfield, Missouri. For information on visiting Rocky Ridge Farm or on becoming a member of the Laura Ingalls Wilder–Rose Wilder Lane Home Association, please write to the Association at Rt. 1, Box 24, Mansfield, MO 65704.

Recipes tested and updated by Mary Kate Morgan

Cover photograph: Picnic on the front lawn of Rocky Ridge Farm
Photograph, preceding page: Looking out the front door of Rocky Ridge farmhouse
Photograph, facing page: Laura Ingalls Wilder, around 1906
Photograph, back cover: Apples on the farmhouse porch steps

The Laura Ingalls Wilder Country Cookbook
Commentary copyright © 1995 by William T. Anderson
Recipe collection copyright © 1995 by Roger Lea MacBride
Illustrations copyright © 1995 by Leslie A. Kelly

HarperCollins®, ♨®, and Little House® are trademarks of HarperCollins Publishers Inc.

Library of Congress Cataloging-in-Publication Data
Wilder, Laura Ingalls, 1867–1957.
  The Laura Ingalls Wilder country cookbook / compiled by Laura Ingalls Wilder ;
commentary by William T. Anderson ; photographs by Leslie A. Kelly.
    p.   cm.
  ISBN 0-06-024917-X.
  1. Cookery, American—Juvenile literature.   2. Wilder, Laura Ingalls, 1867–1957.—Juvenile literature.
[1. Cookery, American.   2. Wilder, Laura Ingalls, 1867–1957.]   I. Anderson, William, date.   II. Kelly, Leslie A., ill.
III. Title.
TX715.W6592   1995   94-42326
641.5973—dc20   CIP
                                                                                                            AC

Typography by Alicia Mikles   2   3   4   5   6   7   8   9   10   ❖

The Laura Ingalls Wilder Country
COOKBOOK

Compiled by *Laura Ingalls Wilder*

COMMENTARY BY WILLIAM ANDERSON
PHOTOGRAPHS BY LESLIE A. KELLY

HarperCollins*Publishers*

Contents

Rocky Ridge Farm, autumn view

Introduction

For generations, readers around the world have been captivated by Laura Ingalls Wilder's account of pioneering life on America's frontier. When she was a farm woman in her sixties, Laura started to pencil recollections of her family's experiences as pioneers and homesteaders. In what became her Little House saga, she told the tale of a covered-wagon trek that began in the Wisconsin forests, extended to the prairies, and was completed with a final move to the Ozark Mountains of Missouri. In 1894, those wagon wheels stopped for twenty-seven-year-old Laura at the door of a log cabin on a knoll near Mansfield, Missouri. Her pioneer years were finished. With her husband, Almanzo, and their seven-year-old daughter, Rose, Laura carved a home from the Missouri land that she named Rocky Ridge Farm.

The farm flourished and their dream house was built. Laura Ingalls Wilder became well known in the Ozarks as a farm activist, a poultry expert, a country columnist, and a jolly hostess. Her neighborly qualities and her efforts to enhance life for rural families endeared her to people in the Mansfield region. When the success of her Little House books transformed her from "Mrs. A. J. Wilder" to the celebrated author Laura Ingalls Wilder, it pleased her that among her peers she was thought of as simply a trusted friend and neighbor. "I am glad that my books have helped children," was her simple response to a celebrity that brought her honors, medals, bags of admiring mail, and a constant stream of friendly visitors.

In 1957, at the age of ninety, Laura died in the farmhouse where she had lived with her beloved Almanzo for most of her life. Even after her death, her fame increased and the curious came to see the house that had given life to the Little House books.

Today, just as Laura's callers of another era were wont to do, visitors first step into the house through the kitchen door. The kitchen provides a cheery welcome; it is bright with sunlight, yellow paint, and vivid red designs on the wallpaper. The cookware, the cheerful potholders on the woodstove, and the colorful dishes create the backdrop for the room where Laura cooked, entertained neighbors, and sometimes opened tablets on the kitchen table to write her stories. The kitchen was the centerpiece of Laura's life during her long years of homemaking.

Until recently, the key to Laura's cooking—her recipes—lay lost among reams of the yellowed papers that are witness to her writing life. But when her home-made cookbook appeared, waterlogged and wrinkled, the pages conjured up the smells, tastes, and textures of her legendary meals.

The Wilders were extraordinary in their thrift and ingenious in recycling useful items. Laura's cookbook exemplifies her careful economy. The cookbook she compiled was actually a scrapbook. Recipes were pasted over pages of a cardboard-covered invoice book used by Almanzo

Laura's recipe notebook

while he was a fuel oil deliveryman in the early 1900s. Internal evidence suggests that the bulk of the cookbook was assembled by Laura during the 1930s and 1940s. On some pages, Laura carefully penned ingredients and cooking instructions. On others she pasted clippings from newspaper food columns, or from magazines like *The Country Gentleman*. She jotted down ideas for meals on the reverse of letters from her New York literary agent. A bread recipe was penciled over an August 1942 calendar leaf. Blank space on a fan letter from a boy in Battle Creek allowed Laura room to record "the way to set colors so goods won't fade." Pages of the cookbook include cooking advice gathered from her mother, Caroline Ingalls, and her daughter, Rose Wilder Lane.

The foodways revealed in Laura's cookbook are what her readers might expect: old-fashioned favorites of an experienced country cook. The recipes she consulted called for foods gleaned from her kitchen garden and staples she kept in her cupboards: cornmeal, brown sugar, white sugar, spices, whole wheat flour, and white flour. More unusual recipes reflect Laura's adventurous spirit. Her recipes indicate her ambition to concoct meals with a foreign flavor for family and friends. Such exotic examples include French bread, brioche, Creole chicken gumbo, and a Portuguese pork pie with oysters. But such fillips are surprising; more predictable are Laura's meat loafs, her corn and bean dishes, filling apple desserts, and her "miracle" rolls.

Each of the recipes in this book has been rigorously tested and updated for the modern kitchen. Most of Laura's cooking was accomplished with a wood-burning cookstove, so even recipes like her much-loved gingerbread have been slightly altered for the convenience of today's cooks.

These recipes from *The Laura Ingalls Wilder Country Cookbook* comprise a patchwork quilt of foodways. They are another surprise from Laura, a gift to her readers as she opens the door into her farm kitchen.

The kitchen at Rocky Ridge farmhouse

Main Dishes

Meat Loaf Supreme

Farmhouse Stew

Chilled Meat Loaf

American Chili

Almanzo's Favorite Swiss Steak

Irish Stew

Golden Pork Chops

Pork Pie with Sweet Potato Biscuits

Ham Loaf with Raisin Sauce

Macaroni Casserole

Liver Loaf

Rose's Famous Chicken Pie

Creole Chicken Gumbo

Old-fashioned Chicken and Dumplings

Chicken Loaf

Salmon Casserole

Salmon Patties

Onion Pie

Cheese Soufflé Supreme

Ingalls family heirlooms on display at Rocky Ridge Farm

Laura Ingalls Wilder's childhood was spent on the frontier during the last phase of American westward expansion. During the 1870s and 1880s, her parents, Charles and Caroline Ingalls, led their family on a search for a permanent home that started in the forests of Wisconsin and concluded on the South Dakota plains. Laura once summed up these travels as follows: "I was born on February 7 in the year 1867 in the Little House in the Big Woods of Wisconsin. From there, with my parents and sisters, I traveled in a prairie schooner across Minnesota, Iowa, Missouri and Kansas, and into Indian Territory, where we lived in the Little House on the Prairie. Then traveling back to western Minnesota we lived for several years on the banks of Plum Creek. From there we went West again, to the shores of Silver Lake in Dakota Territory. We lived in De Smet, the Little Town on the Prairie, and I married Almanzo Wilder in 1885."

Meat Loaf Supreme

*C*hoose your sausage for the flavor you want to give the meat loaf: Italian, sage, spicy . . .

1½ pounds lean chopped beef
½ pound pork sausage (if links,
  remove from casings)
1 egg, beaten
1 cup milk
1 cup fresh bread crumbs

1 medium onion, chopped fine
  (about ¾ cup)
1 teaspoon salt
¼ teaspoon pepper
1 (8-ounce) can mushrooms,
  drained

1. Preheat oven to 375°.

2. Combine all ingredients except mushrooms. Form into loaf shape and place in greased 9½ x 5 x 2-inch loaf pan.

3. Bake for 40 minutes, uncovered, until meat loaf is firm in center.

4. Spread mushrooms over top of meat loaf and bake an additional 30 minutes.

After teaching in country schools on the Dakota prairie, Laura Ingalls married homesteader Almanzo Wilder in 1885. Their first home together was a gray frame house on their homestead land near De Smet. Those early married years were challenging ones for Laura; her book *The First Four Years* describes the crop failures, illnesses, weather extremes, and destruction of her home by fire. The Wilders' daughter, Rose, was born in 1886; in 1889 a son was born and died as an infant. As a young matron in her twenties, Laura put into practice the homemaking activities she had observed from her mother. In addition to preserving and preparing food for her own family, Laura learned to cook in quantity for threshing crews, care for hens and cows, raise a garden, and become an expert seamstress. Laura's early interest in writing down her thoughts and creating original poetry had to be put aside during her first years of homemaking. But she was always a persistent and copious collector of notes and useful information. Penciled jottings during the first years of her married life recorded household tips, recipes, and "beautifying" techniques that a farm woman could practice for hair and complexion.

Farmhouse Stew

*T*his is a thrifty dish. Stretch it by adding a few carrots cut into "pennies" and an extra potato.

*5 medium potatoes, peeled and cut
    into 1-inch cubes
1 quart milk
1 medium onion, minced
4 ribs celery, minced
1½ pounds lean ground beef*

*1 teaspoon salt
½ teaspoon white pepper
3 teaspoons poultry seasoning
3 tablespoons flour mixed into ½
    cup water*

1. Preheat oven to 400°.

2. Combine potatoes, milk, and vegetables in large pot and bring to a boil. Turn heat down and simmer slowly.

3. Prepare meatballs: Mix ground beef and seasonings and form into about 24 small balls. Put on rimmed cookie sheet and bake until browned, about 10 to 12 minutes. Pour off any fat before adding meatballs and juices to simmering stew.

4. Simmer stew for 1 hour. Taste for seasoning and add more salt and pepper if needed. Stir in flour and water mixture and cook 5 minutes longer or until thickened.

Rocky Ridge farmhouse

T his is where we stop," Laura Ingalls Wilder declared as she, her husband, Almanzo, and their daughter, Rose, drove their covered wagon into the little town of Mansfield, Missouri, at summer's end, 1894. Their 650-mile journey from Dakota Territory was complete, and at twenty-seven, Laura Wilder's pioneering ended. Mansfield remained her home for the next sixty-three years. A secreted $100 bill was spent to make a down payment on a farm in the Ozarks. After scouting the neighborhood the Wilders bought a neglected forty-acre plot a mile from the Mansfield town square. The land was a crazy quilt of gullies, knobs, slopes, and slants. Tall timber and thick underbrush covered the place. A limestone rock formation stood sentinel in a deep ravine. Clear water seeped from its ledges into a pool and fed the creek that followed the base of a rounded hill. At the hill's summit stood a log cabin, the Wilder family's new home. Laura responded to the land's lure with a poetic response: she named it Rocky Ridge Farm.

Chilled Meat Loaf

8 SERVINGS

*T*his is elegant enough to be called a terrine! Lovely for a picnic.

*1 piece each pork and beef on the
    bone (about 2 pounds meat)*
2 cups chopped celery tops
1 cup sliced onion
*¼ cup chopped parsley, plus sprigs
    for garnish*

1 tablespoon salt
1 teaspoon pepper
1 envelope unflavored gelatin

1. Place meat and bones in large pot with celery tops, onions, parsley, salt, and pepper, adding enough water to barely cover. Simmer until meat falls from bone, approximately 2 to 3 hours. Strain, reserving broth. Cool.

2. With your fingers, break up meat into coarse pieces and shreds, removing bones and vegetables. You will have about 4 cups of meat. Put meat into greased loaf pan or mold.

3. Remove as much fat as possible from broth. Boil broth until it is reduced to 3 cups. Remove from heat and sprinkle gelatin into broth; stir until dissolved. Pour hot broth over meat, cover and chill loaf overnight.

4. To serve, cut into thin slices and garnish with parsley sprigs.

Sunrise in the Ozarks

The log cabin on Rocky Ridge Farm was a crude new home for Laura, Almanzo, and Rose. Almanzo patched the leaky roof and chinked the gaping cracks between the log walls and Laura made the place cozy. The cabin reminded her of childhood in the Big Woods of Wisconsin, when her family lived in a house of logs with a rock fireplace at one end. The Wilders loved nature and spent much of their time outdoors exploring their land. They walked through the oak woods, used tough grapevines as swings, picnicked in the shady ravine, and waded in the flowing creek. Often they spied treasures along their pathways—curious stones, ancient fossils, and Indian artifacts. In Almanzo's estimation, Laura "had taken a violent fancy to this particular piece of land." Almanzo was always patient with his wife, but he was also practical. "It needed the eye of faith to see that in time it could be made very beautiful," he admitted.

American Chili

*T*here are so many ways to serve chili. Try it over rice with a garnish of chopped lettuce and tomato, or over spaghetti with a dollop of sour cream.

2 pounds ground beef
2–4 onions, minced
2–4 chili peppers, minced
2 cloves garlic, minced
2 tablespoons chili powder or more,
*   to taste*
3 tablespoons paprika
1 tablespoon salt

1 (15-ounce) can tomato sauce
2 (15-ounce) cans red kidney beans
*   with their liquid, or 2 cups dry*
*   kidney beans, soaked overnight,*
*   drained and cooked in water to*
*   cover until tender, about 1½ to*
*   2 hours*

1. Brown meat in large heavy skillet and drain off most of the fat.

2. Add the onions, peppers, and garlic and cook over medium heat until onions are transparent, about 10 minutes. Add remaining ingredients except beans and enough water to barely cover and simmer for 1 hour.

3. Add the beans with any juice and cook until not too soupy.

4. Taste and add more chili powder if needed before serving.

Almanzo Wilder, Neta Seal, Laura Ingalls Wilder
in Yellowstone Park, May 1938

Neta and Silas Seal, a hardworking young Mansfield couple, became Almanzo and Laura's surrogate family during their later years. Rose, who lived in far-off New England, appreciated the love and care the Seals lavished on her parents. "They considered Neta and Silas their children," Rose said. Together, the four friends enjoyed frequent visits, meals, and trips together with Silas doing the driving. He chauffeured them to Detroit in 1937 so that Laura could appear at a book fair sponsored by the J. L. Hudson department store. In 1938, they made a leisurely car trip to California and the Pacific Northwest. On the return trip they stopped at the Wilders' old home in De Smet, South Dakota. It became tradition for Neta to prepare a special dinner for the Wilders' February birthdays. The menu seldom varied: Neta cooked Almanzo's favorite Swiss steak. Almanzo once said to Neta, "Bessie says I brag on your cooking too much, so I won't say anything this time. But you understand: *I'm enjoying it, even if I don't say so!*"

Almanzo's Favorite Swiss Steak

*T*ry Almanzo's favorite dinner for yourself!

½ cup flour
1 teaspoon salt
½ teaspoon freshly ground pepper
2–3 pounds round steak, 1½
    inches thick
2 tablespoons butter

2 tablespoons oil
2 cloves garlic, chopped
1 can condensed cream of
    mushroom soup, diluted
    with 2 cans milk or water

1. Combine flour and seasonings.

2. Pound the flour into both sides of the steak and let stand for ½ hour.

3. Heat butter and oil in large skillet. Brown steak on both sides. Add garlic and cook for a minute.

4. Add soup and simmer for 1 to 2 hours, until meat is tender. Cooking time will depend upon thickness and tenderness of the meat.

Detail of Rocky Ridge farmhouse chimney

Almanzo Wilder, known as "Manly" to family and friends, realized in 1894 that the raw, undeveloped Rocky Ridge Farm would require years of nurture before it returned a profit. He scouted wage-earning possibilities in Mansfield, and the first income came from loads of firewood that Almanzo sold for seventy-five cents. In the late 1890s Almanzo started a draying service in town, hauling goods delivered by train to businesses and individuals in Mansfield, south to Ava, and north to the county seat of Hartville. After the turn of the century, Almanzo Wilder became the delivery agent for the Waters Pierce Oil Company, and followed a regular route through the countryside with supplies of stove gas, kerosene, turpentine, and linseed oil. Almanzo's income enabled him to improve Rocky Ridge, and his dray service allowed him to work with his favorite hobby, horses. His horses were spirited ones, and some of his teams charged through Mansfield so fast that the town marshal warned that they exceeded the speed limits. Before the advent of automobiles there had been no speed limits, Almanzo liked to point out.

Irish Stew

*U*se an inexpensive cut of meat here . . . it will be tender after simmering awhile.

1½ pounds boneless lamb or beef,
cut in 1-inch cubes
Salt, pepper, and paprika
1 cup flour
3 tablespoons olive oil
1 onion, peeled and sliced

4 medium potatoes, peeled and
quartered
4 carrots, peeled and halved
3 parsnips, peeled and halved
½ cup cold water

1. Season meat with salt, pepper, and paprika and pat with flour until meat is well coated. Save unused flour.

2. Heat oil in a heavy skillet and brown meat in three batches, removing when browned. Add onion to skillet and cook briefly, until onion begins to soften.

3. Return meat to pan and add water to cover. Simmer, covered, until meat is almost tender, about 1½ hours.

4. Add vegetables, pressing them down into liquid. Cover and continue to cook until vegetables are done, about 30 minutes.

5. Stir 2 tablespoons reserved flour into ½ cup cold water until dissolved and add gradually to simmering stew, stirring. Cook 5 minutes more, or until thickened.

Wildflowers in an Ozarks meadow

When the Wilders settled on Rocky Ridge Farm in 1894, the nearest school for Rose to attend was in Mansfield, a mile away. Daily she set out, with books and lunch bucket in hand. At first, the lunches were plain fare. The Wilders were too poor to own a cow, so Rose's brown bread was butterless. But Laura often managed to contrive a surprise for her daughter's school lunch. Sometimes the treat was simple: a carrot or an apple; more rarely, because sugar was costly, Laura packed a saucer-sized pie for Rose. "On such occasions," Rose recalled, "she always told me there was a surprise and it was a point of honor not to open the pail until noon, in order to have all morning the delicious anticipation of the unknown." Laura said, "Putting up a school lunch or cooking a good meal for the family may seem very insignificant as compared with giving a lecture or writing a book, but I doubt very much if, in the ultimate reckoning, they will count for as much."

Golden Pork Chops

*C*ooking the pork chops in milk gives them a rich, buttery texture.

4 pork chops, ½ inch thick
Salt and pepper
1 egg, beaten

½ cup cracker crumbs, more or less
1 tablespoon olive oil
2 cups milk, more or less

1. Season pork chops with salt and pepper and dip in egg to moisten all over. Coat with cracker crumbs.

2. Preheat oven to 350°.

3. Heat olive oil in a heavy skillet. Add the pork chops and brown slowly. When golden, add milk to almost cover meat and place in oven. Bake 45 minutes to 1 hour, turning meat once or twice until milk is almost cooked away.

4. Serve immediately, spooning any remaining juices over meat.

Pork Pie with Sweet Potato Biscuits

*T*his unusual combination of ingredients with a Portuguese influence is very tasty. Use leftover pork roast or simmer about 1½ pounds of cubed boneless pork in a little chicken broth until forktender.

1 tablespoon olive oil
2 tablespoons minced onion
2–3 cups finely cubed cooked pork
1 cup pork gravy or broth in which pork was cooked
1 (8-ounce) can oysters, with liquid, or 1 pint oysters and their juice
2 carrots, sliced thin
½ cup diced celery

½ cup chopped celery leaves
1 bay leaf
1 teaspoon salt
½ teaspoon pepper
1 teaspoon rubbed sage
2 cups cooked cubed potatoes
Sweet Potato Biscuits dough (see recipe on facing page)

1. Preheat oven to 425°.

2. Heat oil in large ovenproof skillet. Cook onion over medium heat for 8 to 10 minutes until transparent. Add pork, gravy or broth, oyster juice, carrots, celery, celery leaves, and seasonings.

3. Simmer about ½ hour until vegetables are soft; add potatoes. Simmer a minute or two. Remove bay leaf.

4. Place oysters on top of hot mixture, cover with squares of biscuit dough, and bake 15 to 20 minutes until biscuits are beginning to brown.

Sweet Potato Biscuits

18 BISCUITS

1½ cups flour
2 tablespoons baking powder
¾ tablespoon salt
½ cup cold lard

½ cup milk, if needed
1½ cups drained canned sweet
    potatoes, mashed

1. Sift dry ingredients. Cut in lard.

2. Mix milk into potatoes unless they are very moist already.

3. Stir ingredients together just until mixed. Pat out into ½-inch thickness and cut into square biscuits and place on simmering pie, or drop by heaping tablespoonfuls on simmering pie. If you prefer, you may arrange biscuits on a greased cookie sheet and bake in a preheated 425° oven for 18 to 22 minutes until firm and browned lightly.

A rabbit in an Ozarks meadow

Ham Loaf with Raisin Sauce

*E*ven people who don't care for meat loaf like this one!

1 cup brown sugar
1 teaspoon dry mustard
1 cup apple cider vinegar
½ cup water
1½ pounds ground ham (about 6 cups)
1 pound ground pork

½ teaspoon white pepper
2 eggs, beaten
½ cup drained and coarsely chopped canned tomatoes
⅔ cup milk
1 cup fine cracker crumbs
Raisin Sauce (see recipe on facing page)

1. Make basting sauce: Combine brown sugar, dry mustard, vinegar, and water in a medium saucepan. Bring to a boil and stir until sugar is dissolved, about 2 to 3 minutes.

2. Preheat oven to 350°.

3. Mix all remaining ingredients except raisin sauce and form into loaf shape. Place in greased 9½ x 5 x 2-inch loaf pan.

4. Bake for 1½ hours, basting every 15 minutes with sauce until loaf is lightly browned and firm to touch.

5. When done, remove from oven and allow to stand for 10 or 15 minutes for easier slicing. Serve hot with raisin sauce.

Raisin Sauce

*T*his keeps forever in the refrigerator. It is so delicious!

1 cup granulated sugar	*½ teaspoon Worcestershire sauce*
½ cup water	*½ teaspoon salt*
1 cup raisins	*½ teaspoon pepper*
2 tablespoons butter	*½ teaspoon ground cloves*
3 tablespoons apple cider vinegar	*1 (12-ounce) jar currant jelly*

1. Cook sugar and water 5 minutes over medium heat. Sugar will be completely dissolved.

2. Add remaining ingredients and cook until the jelly is dissolved.

The dining room at Rocky Ridge farmhouse

A comfortable corner of the farmhouse living room

T he house on Rocky Ridge Farm was the result of evolution," said Laura of the ten-room home that grew up around the log cabin her family first occupied. Nearly twenty years elapsed from that first house to the completion of the Wilder home. When additions were made to the original house the Wilders built on their land, Almanzo simply told Laura to "Draw the plans!" Laura's dream house included an oak-beamed and paneled parlor, a library, a writing study, and an open staircase. The house was mostly constructed from materials found on the farm. When it was finished, Laura noted that "It seems to belong on the low hill where it stands, with the tree-covered mountain at its back."

Macaroni Casserole

*T*his would also be tasty made with chopped beef or sausage. Cook and drain the fat off before you combine with the meat sauce.

3 tablespoons butter
⅓ cup chopped onion
⅓ cup chopped green pepper
¼ cup flour
3 bouillon cubes dissolved in 2 cups boiling water, or 2 cups chicken broth
1 cup diced leftover cooked meat or chicken, or diced luncheon meat

2 cups canned tomatoes in their juice
Salt and pepper to taste
1 (8-ounce) package elbow macaroni, cooked and drained
¼ cup fresh bread crumbs

1. Preheat oven to 375°.

2. Heat butter in skillet; add onion and pepper and cook until softened.

3. Blend in flour and stir in bouillon, meat, and tomatoes. Taste and add salt and pepper if desired.

4. Combine macaroni and sauce in buttered ovenproof casserole dish and sprinkle with bread crumbs.

5. Bake for 30 minutes or until casserole is bubbling and crumbs are brown.

Upstairs window of the farmhouse

While waiting for Rocky Ridge Farm to become a paying proposition, the Wilders lived in Mansfield. By 1898 they were settled in a yellow cottage at the edge of town. This became the base for Almanzo's dray service, and it was a short walk to the school Rose attended. For Laura, the move to town gave her a chance to earn some income. In her dining room she served well-prepared meals to boarders. The officials of the Bluebird Railroad, the town banker, and other hungry passersby all became regulars at Laura's table. Later, when the house on Rocky Ridge was completed and the Wilders returned to the farm to live, Laura continued to offer her hospitality to paying guests. She filled empty bedrooms with "summer boarders," mostly refugees from the hot cities who arrived to take a "rest cure" in the country. "Nearly all that is needed to make a delightful bill of fare is produced right on the farm," Laura noted. She found that she could "earn a tidy sum" through her meals and hospitality. And for Laura there was an added bonus in opening her home to boarders. "Some of my dearest friends are among the people whom I first met in this way," she said.

Liver Loaf

6 MAIN COURSE SERVINGS
12 APPETIZER SERVINGS

*T*his is very nice. If used as an appetizer, garnish with sour pickle slices.

1 pound beef liver
1 cup milk
1 cup bread crumbs
2 tablespoons ketchup
¼ cup finely chopped onion

1 egg, beaten
Juice of 1 lemon (about 3–4 table-
spoons)
1 teaspoon salt
6–8 strips bacon

1. Soak liver in milk for 1 hour or longer. Discard milk. Trim membranes from liver and poach in boiling salted water for 5 minutes.

2. Preheat oven to 350°.

3. Cut liver into 1-inch pieces and process in food processor until smooth. Add remaining ingredients except bacon and process until well combined.

4. Line a small greased loaf pan with strips of bacon. Pack liver mixture into pan and top with strips of bacon. Wrap pan with foil, sealing completely.

5. Put loaf pan into a shallow pan of water and bake for 1½ hours.

6. Loosen foil and pour off any accumulated fat from loaf pan.

7. This may be served hot or at room temperature. Serve in slivers as a main course or an appetizer.

Rose's Famous Chicken Pie

*T*here's no question about it—this is *the* best chicken pie! This recipe may be prepared over a couple of days. There are two time-consuming steps: the frying and cooling. About 2 hours before serving time, remove the casserole from the refrigerator and dinner is almost ready!

1 roasting chicken, the largest you can get, cut into serving-size pieces

2 cups flour, plus ¼ cup to thicken gravy

1½ cups oil (or more) for sautéing chicken

1 large onion, diced

1 tablespoon salt

1 teaspoon pepper

2 cups flour

2 heaping teaspoons baking powder

2 teaspoons salt

2 teaspoons granulated sugar

1 egg

1⅓ cups heavy cream

1. Coat chicken with flour. Reserve unused flour for making gravy. Heat ½ cup oil in iron skillet: brown chicken a few pieces at a time, adding more oil as needed. Remove each browned piece to large pot, along with backbone and giblets. Save the liver for another use.

2. Add onion, salt, and pepper to the pot of chicken and cover all with boiling water. Simmer, covered, until chicken is very tender, about 2 hours. Cool in broth. It can be refrigerated at this point.

3. Remove as much fat from the pot as you can; save it for the gravy. Remove chicken pieces from the broth, discarding the backbone and giblets. The pie can be made with chicken on the bone, or you can remove the skin and bone and use meat only. Place chicken in large ovenproof casserole, white meat on one side, dark meat on the other, and wings in center.

4. To make the gravy, measure 1 tablespoon fat and 1½ tablespoons flour for each cup of broth (8 to 10 cups of broth will provide plenty of gravy). Use the flour left over from dredging plus additional flour if necessary.

5. Warm the fat in a skillet. Stir in flour until thoroughly mixed and whisk in broth. Simmer, stirring, until thickened and smooth. Pour over chicken. Cover casserole and refrigerate until ready to bake.

6. One and a half hours before serving, place covered casserole in preheated 300° oven for 40 minutes to heat contents until bubbling.

7. Meanwhile, sift together 2 cups flour, baking powder, sugar, and salt. Mix together egg and cream. Just before you remove casserole from oven, stir flour and egg mixture to just combine. Do not beat. Uncover casserole and place spoonfuls of dough all around edge, scraping spoon outward on dish to seal dough to edge. All gravy does not need to be covered. Place casserole on cookie sheet to catch drips. Return to oven as quickly as possible. Biscuits should be nicely browned in about 20 minutes.

8. This can be served at once or can be held in turned-off oven for ½ hour or so. To serve, place portion of biscuit on plate, upside down, and spoon chicken and gravy over.

Rose Wilder Lane

Ozarks farmland

G osh! Sure was a happy childhood," exclaimed Almanzo Wilder as he thought of his boyhood on the family farm near Malone, New York. Almanzo's memories became the pages of his wife's book *Farmer Boy* (HarperCollins, 1933). As a boy Almanzo learned the ways of operating a typical mixed-product New England farm. As a homesteader in De Smet, Dakota Territory, Almanzo struggled to become a successful wheat farmer on 320 acres of prairie land, but the attempt never paid off. (See *The First Four Years*.) After settling in Mansfield, Missouri, Almanzo returned to farming practices he had known as a boy. On his Rocky Ridge Farm, he plowed assorted fields: he raised cattle, sheep, poultry, Morgan horses, and grew fruit and diverse crops. The approach became profitable. "Mr. Wilder is one of our most progressive farmers," noted the local newspaper in 1913.

Creole Chicken Gumbo

A delicious variation of stewed chicken. Serve with plain boiled rice.

½ pound ham or sausage, diced
1 (4–5-pound) roasting chicken, cut
  into serving pieces
2 onions, minced
1 (1-pound) package frozen okra,
  thawed and sliced
2 tablespoons flour

Butter, if needed, for cooking okra
3 quarts boiling water
1 (28-ounce) can plum tomatoes
  with their juices
1 bay leaf
1 teaspoon hot sauce
Salt to taste

1. Sauté ham slowly in large skillet, until fat is melted out of meat. Remove meat to large soup pot, leaving fat in pan.

2. Add chicken to skillet and brown slowly in ham fat until golden brown on both sides. Cook chicken in batches if necessary. Remove to soup pot.

3. Add the onions and okra to the skillet. Stir in flour and cook over low heat for about 25 minutes, stirring often and adding butter or water if necessary to keep from sticking. Transfer vegetables to soup pot. Add about ¾ cup boiling water to pan and scrape to loosen any bits of meat or vegetables. Add this to soup pot with remaining boiling water and the tomatoes.

4. Add bay leaf and hot sauce to pot and bring to a boil. Reduce heat and simmer slowly for 2 hours, stirring often.

5. Taste for seasoning and remove bay leaf.

Rocky Ridge farmhouse in the moonlight

Over the fence to the farmhouse,
With laughter and repartee gay,
It's almost time to be eating again
And we're rather too far away.
There's chicken and dumplings for dinner,
With salads and vegetables fine
And fruits just fresh from the orchard
Oh who wouldn't love to dine!
Over the fence to the farmhouse,
We're afraid they will not wait
And with chicken and dumplings for dinner
'Twould never do to be late.

—Laura Ingalls Wilder

Old-fashioned Chicken and Dumplings

*T*his is a favorite Sunday dinner.

1 large roasting or stewing chicken,	*2 eggs*
cut in pieces	*⅔ cup milk*
1 rib celery with leaves, cut fine	*3 teaspoons baking powder*
1 or 2 carrots, sliced thin	*2 cups flour, plus ¼ cup to thicken*
3 teaspoons salt (divided use)	*gravy*
½ teaspoon freshly grated pepper	*2 tablespoons butter*
½ teaspoon mace	

1. Arrange chicken pieces in large pot; add vegetables, 2 teaspoons salt, pepper, mace, and water to cover by at least an inch. (You need plenty of broth to cook the dumplings.) Bring to a boil, reduce heat, and simmer until chicken is tender, about 1½ hours.

2. Place cooked chicken pieces in an ovenproof dish. You may remove the bones if you wish. Cover and keep warm.

3. Make the dumpling batter: Mix the eggs, 1 teaspoon salt, and milk together. Sift the dry ingredients. Cut butter into flour with two knives or a pastry cutter. Blend the wet and dry ingredients to a fairly stiff dough, adding a little more flour if needed.

4. Drop the dough by spoonfuls into the boiling broth. Cover the pot tightly, reduce the heat slightly to prevent boiling, and cook for 15 minutes *without removing the cover.*

5. To serve, arrange the chicken and dumplings on a hot platter with a little of the hot broth. Serve extra broth separately or make gravy by slowly mixing ¼ cup flour into 1 cup of the broth. Return it to the simmering broth and cook for 5 minutes, stirring.

A corner of the farmhouse kitchen

In her role as housekeeper, Laura was always interested in modern innovations and laborsaving devices. The kitchen on Rocky Ridge became a testimony to her practicality and creative energy. The kitchen was remodeled, and modernized many times through the years. Around 1920, the kitchen was moved to an adjoining woodshed, leaving space for a new dining room. In the process Laura was determined to create a customized working place with a minimum of expense. She planned and Almanzo worked on the project between farm chores. They finished the work in a year and spent just $49.84 to complete the job. Laura described the newly made kitchen as a combination of cabinets and windows. In an era when built-in cupboards were a rarity, Laura insisted on them. Countertops were low-slung to accommodate her five-foot stature. Window seats lifted to reveal storage bins for staples. A pass-through next to the sink connected the kitchen and dining room. Without taking a step, Laura could pass food and dishes on to the dining table and easily collect the remainders following the meal. When Laura painted the whole kitchen with dazzling white enamel, she pronounced it a job well done. "The convenience and whiteness are a continual joy," she said proudly. "It is a kitchen to be happy in."

Chicken Loaf

*T*his is a very bland loaf. Give it your own seasoning personality!

4 cups diced cooked chicken
2 cups fresh bread crumbs
2 tablespoons chopped parsley
2 tablespoons chopped green pepper
2 tablespoons chopped celery
1 teaspoon salt

1 teaspoon paprika
4 eggs, beaten
3 cups milk
1–2 tablespoons chopped fresh
   herbs—your choice. Tarragon is
   always good.

1. Preheat oven to 350°.

2. Combine all ingredients and spoon into buttered medium ovenproof dish.

3. Bake for 1 hour until center is firm.

Laura picking peas in her Rocky Ridge garden

Long after the lands of Rocky Ridge ceased to be active farmland, Laura and Almanzo continued to plant a kitchen garden. "All summer we gather fresh vegetables and berries from our garden," Laura said, "and in the fall we gather walnuts and pecans from our own trees." In the fall of 1947, artist Garth Williams arrived at Rocky Ridge to visit the Wilders and discuss illustrations for the Little House books. At the driveway gate he spied Laura, age eighty, working vigorously in the garden. "I stopped to watch her," Garth recalled. "She was sprightly, very much alive and without a doubt the Laura of her books. She was small and nimble. Her eyes sparkled with good humor and she seemed a good twenty years younger than her age. She took us into the house and we looked at all her old family photographs. She told us about the people and just where to find Plum Creek and all the other places mentioned in the books."

Salmon Casserole

A quick and easy family dinner in one dish. A great way to use leftover mashed potatoes.

2 tablespoons butter
2 tablespoons flour
2 cups milk
Salt and pepper to taste
1 can salmon (about 1¾ cups)
1 (10-ounce) package frozen peas

4 potatoes
Salt, plus 1 teaspoon (divided use)
1 tablespoon butter or margarine
2 or 3 tablespoons milk, or to taste
¼ teaspoon pepper

1. Preheat oven to 350°.

2. Make white sauce: Melt butter over low heat. Blend in flour completely. Whisk in milk and cook until thickened, about 3 to 5 minutes. Season with salt and pepper.

3. Flake salmon into greased 1½-quart ovenproof dish, and cover with peas.

4. Peel, quarter, and cook potatoes in salted water to cover until forktender. Drain.

5. Mash hot cooked potatoes with butter. Add milk a tablespoon at a time until potatoes are free from lumps. They should be fairly stiff in consistency. Season to taste with remaining 1 teaspoon salt and pepper.

6. Pour white sauce over salmon and peas and top with mashed potatoes.

7. Bake for 35 to 45 minutes or until potatoes are beginning to brown.

The Wilders' organ and hymnal

Church life was an important part of each pioneer community in which Laura Ingalls Wilder lived. In Mansfield, she and Almanzo participated in the development of the Methodist church, which held its first service in the congregation's completed building at Christmastime 1899. Laura organized the first bazaar of the Methodist Episcopal Aid Society in Mansfield, and assisted with fund-raising sales and dinners. She described one of them, held in a room over Reynolds' General Store:

> Long tables covered with white cloths were set in the middle of the room. On the tables were plates of white bread and of brown bread, dishes of butter and of pickles and salads of different kinds. People were coming and going at these tables while the cashier of the Aid Society hovered near, collecting the price of the dinner. In an improvised kitchen, at the back of the room, the older women were dishing up the food on plates which white-aproned girls carried to the diners at the tables. Portions of baked beans, fried or roasted or boiled chicken, with gravy, mashed potatoes, candied sweet potatoes and boiled ham were put on each plate. A cup of coffee and a piece of pie were also served to each guest.

Whether at home in her own kitchen, or when cooking for fund-raising events, Laura's food was a welcomed addition to meals.

Salmon Patties

*T*his can also be made with fresh salmon. Just barely cook it in a little water or white wine, flake it and remove the bones.

4 potatoes	*1 egg, beaten*
Salt, plus 1 teaspoon (divided use)	*1 (1-pound) can salmon, bones*
1 tablespoon butter	*removed*
2 or 3 tablespoons milk, or to taste	*Salt and pepper to taste*
¼ teaspoon pepper	*Butter or oil*

1. Peel, quarter, and cook potatoes in salted water to cover for about 15 minutes. Drain.

2. Mash hot cooked potatoes with butter. Add milk a tablespoon at a time until potatoes are free from lumps. They should be fairly stiff in consistency. Season to taste with remaining 1 teaspoon salt and pepper.

3. Mix egg into cooled mashed potatoes.

4. Mix salmon into potatoes lightly, keeping small chunks of salmon intact if possible. Season to taste and form into patties.

5. In nonstick frying pan, heat butter or oil. Add patties and fry over medium heat until golden, about 5 minutes. Turn and cook on second side.

Laura Ingalls Wilder, around 1917

In 1911 Laura Ingalls Wilder took her first step from the henhouse to the publishing house. Her Ozarks neighbors had watched her success in poultry raising and envied her ability to make each hen net a dollar in profit. When questioned about her methods, Laura simply said she kept the henhouse immaculate, provided ample fresh water and the right kinds of feed for her fowl. Then invitations started arriving, asking that Laura share her techniques with farmers' meetings and land congress events throughout the Ozarks. Even though she was never comfortable with public speaking, Laura good-naturedly prepared talks to deliver before groups of interested fellow farmers. Once when she was unable to attend a meeting she wrote out her usual speech to be read in absentia. In that particular audience was the editor of the *Missouri Ruralist*, who listened with interest to the words of "Mrs. A. J. Wilder." Soon he contacted Laura, requesting an article from her, and proudly Laura published her first commissioned writing at the age of forty-four.

Onion Pie

With crusty bread and a salad, this makes a nice light supper dish—or try it for a brunch.

4–6 slices bacon
3 cups sliced onions
2 eggs
1 cup whole milk, or ½ milk and ½
*   cream*

Refrigerated unbaked piecrust for
*   10-inch pie*
½ cup grated cheese, your favorite
*   kind*

1. Preheat oven to 350°.

2. Cut bacon slices into small pieces and fry until almost crispy. Add onions and cook over medium heat until onions are wilted but not browned, about 10 to 15 minutes.

3. Combine eggs and milk.

4. Mix onions and milk and pour into pie shell. Top with grated cheese and bake for 30 minutes or until filling is set. You can gently shake the pan back and forth and see if the center is firm.

5. Let cool on rack for a few minutes before cutting into wedges to serve.

Rocky Ridge farmhouse porch in the sunlight

A common thread ran through Laura Ingalls Wilder's early journalism: that life in the country was a good alternative to living in crowded urban areas. She resented the image of a bedraggled countrywoman, uninformed, isolated, and forgotten because she did not live in town. "Wake up to your opportunities!" Laura exhorted farm women. Laura saw a farm home and rural living as a privilege. With creativity, she believed that no farm family should lack anything its city counterparts enjoyed. She spoke with admiration of her own homesite, with its parklike five-acre yard, ancient oak trees, clear running stream, birds, and fresh air. Every farm could develop its own beautiful vistas, according to Laura. To avoid rural isolation, Laura suggested that families band together actively to create their own social and cultural circles. Her own Rocky Ridge Farm was a popular gathering place. "The little farm is a delightful place for friends to come to afternoon tea under the trees," Laura said. "There is room for a tennis court . . . there are skating parties in winter and sewing and reading clubs . . . What more could anyone want?" Laura asked when discussing the charms she found in life on the farm.

Cheese Soufflé Supreme

A French classic.

3 tablespoons butter	*¼ teaspoon white pepper*
¼ cup flour	*½ teaspoon paprika*
1 cup milk	*1 cup grated sharp Cheddar*
½ teaspoon salt	*4 eggs, separated*

1. Melt butter in saucepan, stir in flour, and cook over low heat for 2 to 3 minutes. Add milk slowly, stirring over low heat until sauce thickens. Add seasonings and cheese and continue stirring until cheese is melted. Set aside to cool.

2. Preheat oven to 325°. Grease 6-cup soufflé dish.

3. Beat egg yolks until light in color. Stir into cheese mixture.

4. Beat egg whites until stiff but not dry. Fold into cheese mixture until just mixed.

5. Pour into prepared dish; set dish in pan of boiling water and bake 50 minutes. When done, the soufflé will be well puffed with firm outer edges. The center will wobble slightly when shaken gently. Serve immediately.

Corn resting on the side porch steps of Rocky Ridge farmhouse

Vegetable and Side Dishes

Scalloped Corn Kansas

Missouri Succotash

Glazed Beets

Baked Lettuce

Pilaf

Hush Puppies

Potato Pancakes

Limas Louisiana

Lima Puree Soup

Dandelion Soup

Rocky Ridge farmhouse

The white frame farmhouse where Laura Ingalls Wilder lived near Mansfield, Missouri, was already a landmark in the Ozarks at the time of the author's death in 1957; for years, readers had sought out both the house and its famous resident. Through the generosity of the Wilders' daughter, Rose Wilder Lane, the house and its contents eventually were turned over to the nonprofit Laura Ingalls Wilder Home Association to be preserved and shown to admirers of the Little House books. Rose wrote:

> My mother wished so much that the house could be kept as a memorial . . . She could never quite realize that she was actually famous, to her it did not seem possible that she was; New York and London and Tokyo were too far away to seem quite real . . . Nothing would have pleased her more than knowing that Mansfield people want to keep her house in memory of her.

Scalloped Corn Kansas

*T*his is a custardy side dish—perfect with a roast or even hamburgers!

2 (12–15-ounce) cans whole-kernel
  corn
1½ cups light cream
4 tablespoons butter
4 tablespoons flour

1 teaspoon salt
½ teaspoon white pepper
4 eggs, beaten
1 cup fine dry bread crumbs

1. Preheat oven to 350°. Drain the corn, reserving juice in measuring cup. Add cream to the juice to make 2 cups of liquid.

2. Melt butter in small saucepan. Whisk in flour, salt, and pepper. Add corn-cream liquid and cook over low heat until thickened, stirring constantly. Set aside to cool slightly.

3. Grease shallow 1½-quart baking dish. Combine corn, eggs, and corn-cream liquid; pour into greased baking dish and sprinkle with bread crumbs.

4. Place baking dish in shallow pan of water in oven and bake for 45 to 50 minutes or until center is firm when dish is shaken slightly.

Laura's writing desk

Encouraged by the sale of magazine articles to *The Country Gentleman* in 1925, Laura searched for subject matter suitable to appear in nationally distributed publications. She had long considered writing about her own recollections of pioneer life, but a format never clearly presented itself. But after her success in *The Country Gentleman* Laura decided to write about frontier food-ways. For background information, Laura contacted her Aunt Martha Carpenter, Ma's older sister. "*The Ladies Home Journal* is wanting me to write . . . on our grand-mother's cooking brought down to date," Laura wrote her aunt, who still lived in Pepin, Wisconsin. "I am thinking that you could give me some recipes." Aunt Martha provided Laura with recipes, but more importantly, she recounted her memories of frontier life and encouraged Laura to write of those days. Laura never wrote the article about frontier foods. But Aunt Martha's tales and her own growing desire to write of life as she remembered it took form in the late 1920s.

Missouri Succotash

*U*se vegetables fresh from your garden or your local farm stand.

*1 pound green beans, trimmed and
   cut in 1-inch pieces*
½ teaspoon each salt and pepper
¾ cup water
½ teaspoon granulated sugar

3 medium-size ears fresh corn
½ cup light cream
1 teaspoon finely minced onion
2 tablespoons butter
A few gratings of fresh nutmeg

1. Place the beans and seasonings in a saucepan with water. Boil rapidly until tender—the water should be almost gone, about 8 minutes.

2. Cut the corn from the cob, first slicing off a thin layer, then scraping the cob to get as much pulp as possible. Add to the beans along with the remaining ingredients.

3. Heat together just long enough to cook the corn, about 3 to 5 minutes.

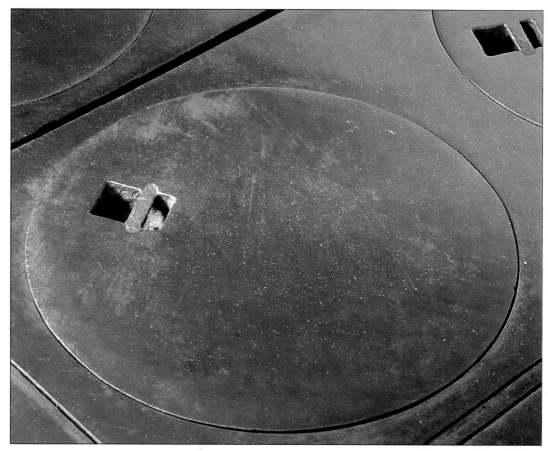

A burner on the farmhouse cookstove

Ahandsome green and cream-colored Montgomery Ward "Blue Ribbon" cookstove presided over the Wilder kitchen, behemoth-style. It was manufactured circa 1905 and served Laura for over a half-century. Its purpose was dual; not only did the wood-burning range cook the meals, it also warmed the kitchen end of the farmhouse. Almanzo constructed a linoleum-topped woodbox to sit near the stove and when he harnessed a hillside spring for a water source in the house, he ran a pipe into the stove. Thus, hot water was available in the stove's reservoir. When the Wilders returned to the farmhouse after living in the nearby rock house, they added a Westinghouse three-burner electric stove in a kitchen corner. This Laura used in the heat of summer, when she didn't choose to fire up the woodstove, or as she said, "When I need to heat a quick bit of hot water." For one who clung to her past, it is not surprising that Laura Wilder always preferred using the cookstove.

Glazed Beets

*Y*ou can cook fresh beets for this or substitute canned ones; either one is good.

3 cups sliced cooked beets
¼ cup granulated sugar
½ teaspoon cinnamon
¼ teaspoon ground cloves
2 tablespoons butter

¼ teaspoon salt
¼ teaspoon pepper
3 tablespoons apple cider vinegar
2 tablespoons water

1. Combine all ingredients in large saucepan.

2. Cover pan and simmer for 15 minutes.

Ozarks farmland

During the height of the farming operation, Laura and Almanzo realized with pleasure that they could raise nearly everything they needed to supply their table on their own land. Only a few supplies were needed from the Mansfield grocery stores. Even after they retired from active farming, Almanzo still raised a big garden and Laura thriftily preserved all the produce she could. During Almanzo's last illness and after his death in 1949, Laura became dependent on a weekly trip to the grocery store to supply her kitchen. Wednesday was her day to shop in Mansfield, because that had been the routine with Almanzo. Jim Hartley, the town taxi driver, took Laura to town for visiting, errands, and groceries. During the 1950s, when royalties from her Little House books were amounting to a prosperous income, Rose once suggested that Laura buy a mink coat. "Now, Rose," Laura reasoned, "wouldn't I look silly sitting on a banana box at the grocery store, waiting for Mr. Hartley to drive me home in a mink coat?"

Baked Lettuce

An elegant addition to a special dinner, it can be prepared and popped into the oven just before dinner.

6 heads Boston lettuce
Water to cover lettuce seasoned with
   1 teaspoon salt
6 tablespoons melted butter
½ teaspoon white pepper

¼ teaspoon freshly grated nutmeg
1 teaspoon salt
2 or 3 tablespoons fine dry bread
   crumbs

1. Soak heads of lettuce in salted water for several hours. Keeping shape intact, remove cores carefully and run water through lettuce to clean completely. Then secure the shape of the head by tying with white string or with a rubber band.

2. Preheat oven to 350°. Bring a pot of water to a strong simmer. Add heads of lettuce and simmer 2 minutes. Remove lettuce and drain thoroughly.

3. Remove string and arrange lettuce in buttered 4-cup baking dish. Spoon butter, salt, pepper, and nutmeg over each head and sprinkle with crumbs.

4. Bake for 15 minutes or until crumbs are browned lightly.

Pilaf

*T*he chicken broth adds flavor and a special touch.

2 tablespoons butter
1 cup converted rice
2 cups chicken broth

1 teaspoon salt, or to taste
½ teaspoon pepper

1. Preheat oven to 350°. Grease 1-quart oven-proof casserole.

2. Melt butter in large skillet. Add rice and sauté about 5 minutes, stirring constantly. Rice will begin to brown.

3. Turn rice into casserole and stir in remaining ingredients. Bake for 30 minutes, stir; bake 30 minutes longer or until rice is tender.

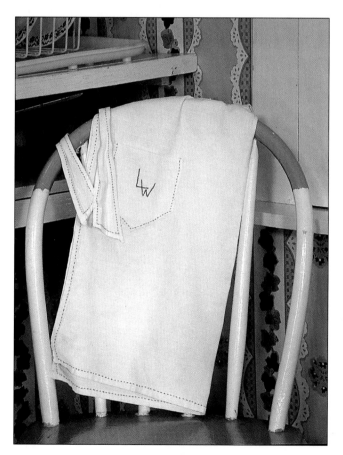

Laura's embroidered apron

Hush Puppies

*C*ook these in oil left from frying fish or chicken for a special flavor.

1 cup cornmeal   *2 eggs*
2 teaspoons baking powder   *⅓ cup milk*
½ teaspoon salt   *Oil for deep frying*
1 medium onion, chopped fine

1. Mix the dry ingredients together and stir in the onion.

2. Beat the eggs and stir in milk. Combine all ingredients immediately before frying.

3. Heat oil to 365° (use a thermometer or drop a teaspoon of batter in—it should start to bubble immediately). Drop tablespoons of batter into oil and cook 5 to 7 minutes or until golden and crispy on both sides. Drain on paper towels and serve hot.

A young Rose at the cave with her donkey, Spookendyke

Life was not intended to be simply a round of work," Laura declared. She and Almanzo learned that quick relief from their daily grind of farmwork could be achieved by a walk in their woods or a picnic dinner among the trees in the ravine behind the house. The Wilders' love of nature led Laura to plan outdoor dining in a variety of beautiful spots around Rocky Ridge Farm. With neighbors, they sometimes ventured to nearby Williams Cave with picnic baskets in hand. Nighttime fox chases always included campfires with coffee boiling and bacon frying over the flames. Longer jaunts took the Wilders to the banks of the Gasconade River near Hartville, where they camped and fried fresh fish caught by Almanzo. Farmers were relentlessly burdened by daily care of their crops and animals, but Laura knew the value of quick, impromptu breaks in the routine. "A moment's pause to watch the glory of a sunrise or a sunset is soul satisfying," she said, "while a bird's song will set the steps to music all day long."

Potato Pancakes

Grate the potatoes just before you use them, as they discolor quickly. Try these with hot applesauce spooned over them.

2 eggs, beaten
2–3 large potatoes, grated (about
   3 cups)

1 tablespoon flour
1 teaspoon salt

1. Preheat heavy griddle or frying pan over low heat. A cast-iron pan is best for this job.

2. Combine all ingredients in large mixing bowl.

3. Grease pan generously with butter, lard, or oil. Ladle out potato mixture in pancake-size portions into frying pan. Cook over medium heat until golden brown and crispy; flip and cook second side.

An autumn tree on Rocky Ridge Farm

Spending her time on a farm focused Laura's own life philosophies. Harvest time prompted her to ponder that "We have been gathering the fruits of the season's work into barns and bins and cellars . . . Now I am wondering what sort of fruits and how plentiful is the supply we have stored in our hearts and minds from the year's activities?" Autumn—harvest time—was Laura's favorite season on the farm. One October she wrote of it: "There is a purple haze over the hilltops and a hint of sadness in the sunshine because of summer's departure; on the low ground down by the spring the walnuts are dropping from the trees and squirrels are busy hiding away their winter supply. Here and there the leaves are beginning to change color and a little vagrant autumn breeze goes wandering over the hills and down the valleys, whispering to 'follow, follow,' until it is almost impossible to resist. So I should not be too harshly criticized if I ramble . . ."

Limas Louisiana

A thrifty winter supper dish.

½ pound pork sausage links	*1 teaspoon salt*
2 cups dried lima beans, cooked	*½ teaspoon poultry seasoning*
¼ cup minced onion	*1 cup milk*
1 teaspoon granulated sugar	*1 tablespoon butter*
¼ teaspoon mace	*¼ cup shredded green pepper*

1. Preheat oven to 350°.

2. Boil sausage links for 5 minutes. Drain.

3. Combine limas, onion, and seasonings in a shallow oiled 1-quart baking dish. Press sausage links onto top of bean mixture.

4. Pour milk over limas. Dot with butter and top with shredded peppers.

5. Bake for 30 minutes.

Cows in an Ozarks pasture

While the careers of Laura and Rose brought renown to the Wilder name in journalism and literature, Almanzo was known as one of Wright County's best farmers. Making Rocky Ridge Farm productive was not an easy task; much of the land was stony and untillable. But Almanzo worked magic with the stubborn soil. The local newspaper, the *Mansfield Mirror*, reported many of Almanzo's successes on the farm. In an agricultural area like Mansfield, readers were interested to know that one of the Wilder cows yielded twenty-four pounds of milk at one milking. "Can you beat that?" asked the newspaper when Almanzo brought in heads of wheat over seven inches long. Almanzo was modest when he produced a fifteen-inch tomato. "Stuff just grows naturally in the Ozarks and you can't help it," he said. When Mansfield started its annual Agricultural and Stock Show, Almanzo was both a judge and a participant. Year after year he won prizes for cows, hens, sheep, and field crop specimens.

Lima Puree Soup

A hearty soup. Add a little diced ham and serve with salad and a crusty bread for a light supper.

2 cups cooked dried lima beans
4 cups chicken broth, or 4 bouillon
cubes dissolved in 4 cups boil-
ing water
Salt and pepper to taste

¼ cup finely minced onion
1 tablespoon soft butter
2 tablespoons flour
½ cup heavy cream (optional)

1. Puree beans in food processor with small amount of chicken broth (to make your soup smoother, press pureed beans through coarse strainer).

2. Transfer puree to medium saucepan and stir in remaining broth, seasonings, and onion. Simmer until onion is tender.

3. Make a paste of the butter and flour. Add a little hot soup and mix until smooth. Add paste to the soup, stirring briskly. Cook 5 minutes or until thickened. Taste for seasoning and add salt and pepper if needed.

4. Serve soup hot with a little puddle of heavy cream floating on top if desired.

One of Laura's Haviland china place settings

Laura and Almanzo were both longtime active members of Mansfield's chapter of the Order of Eastern Star, a religious and charitable organization. They were often instigators of social activities among the membership, as simple as the serving of apples from Almanzo's orchard to a more complicated theme party held at Rocky Ridge in January 1917. In the flowery manner of country journalism of the era, the *Mansfield Mirror* reported the Eastern Star social at the Wilder home . . .

> The invitation was a complete surprise to the chapter members, who had only expected the regular meeting. Three cars conveyed the merry crowd to Rocky Ridge Farm, where the oak paneled, oak beamed living room was alight from the large fireplace and the glow of rose-shaded lamps from the dining room. Delicious and unique refreshments were served . . . the table decorations were in the Star colors, the centerpiece being the regular Star emblem in the correct colors. The edibles served on each plate were also in the proper colors and designs of the Star. After lunch, the guests gathered in the firelight and listened to the wonderful violin music of Kreisler . . . selections from well-known operas, Victor Herbert's orchestra and Hawaiian stringed instruments. The music was furnished by a Victrola, the Christmas gift of Rose Wilder Lane of San Francisco. With music and conversation the time passed without a dull moment and the guests departed, regretting that the evening had been too short.

Dandelion Soup

*Y*ou can pick dandelion leaves in your own yard if you haven't used chemicals! Early spring provides the tender new leaves. If you have a perfect grassy lawn, try an Italian market or a farm stand.

¼ cup butter
1 cup finely chopped dandelion
   leaves
1 tablespoon minced garlic
1 tablespoon minced chives

1 teaspoon salt
½ teaspoon pepper
3 tablespoons flour
4 cups milk

1. Melt butter; add greens, herbs, and seasonings. Sauté for about 10 minutes to cook greens, stirring constantly. Leaves will shrink and soften.

2. Sprinkle in flour, stirring to coat greens evenly. Cook about 5 minutes.

3. Stir in milk, cooking over low heat until smooth. Simmer until greens are tender, approximately 5 minutes. Serve hot.

Bread cooling on the cookstove in the Rocky Ridge kitchen

—60—

Breads and Rolls

Whole Wheat Bread

Miracle Rolls

Brioche

French Bread

Poppy Seed Crescents

Orange Nut Bread

Orange Rolls

Lemon Spice Puffs

Raisin Tea Ring

A winter view of Rocky Ridge Farm

Laura Ingalls Wilder's book *The Long Winter* (HarperCollins, 1940) graphically describes survival during the 1880 to 1881 winter months when deep snows and blizzards isolated the town of De Smet, Dakota Territory. For Laura's family, meals became so spare that a portion of bread was the sole offering. In 1917, Laura wrote of the struggle for daily bread . . .

> The small supply of provisions in town soon gave out. The last sack of flour sold for $50 and the last of the sugar at $1 a pound. There was some wheat on hand, brought in the fall before for seed in the spring, and two young men dared to drive fifteen miles to where a solitary settler had also laid in his supply of seed wheat. They brought it in on sleds. There were no mills in town or country so this wheat was ground in the homes in coffee mills. Everybody ground wheat, even the children taking their turns, and the resultant whole wheat flour made good bread. It was also a healthful food and there was not a case of sickness in town that winter.

Whole Wheat Bread

*T*his is a dark, sweet bread—delicious spread with whipped cream cheese. It keeps well.

½ cup brown sugar
½ cup dark molasses, plus a little
extra if needed
1 egg
¾ teaspoon baking soda dissolved
in 2 tablespoons hot water
1 cup milk

1½ cups whole wheat flour
1½ cups all-purpose flour
2 teaspoons baking powder
1 teaspoon salt
1 cup walnuts
1 cup raisins

1. Preheat oven to 350°. Grease two 8½ x 4½ x 2½-inch loaf pans.

2. Put brown sugar in measuring cup. Add molasses and let it seep into sugar. Add extra molasses if necessary to bring to full cup. Scrape into mixing bowl.

3. Add egg, dissolved baking soda, and milk, stirring well.

4. Sift flours, baking powder, and salt. Combine nuts and raisins and stir in a tablespoon or two of the flour, just so they are lightly coated.

5. Beat flour into the batter; stir in nuts and raisins until evenly distributed. Divide batter between prepared pans.

6. Bake for about 1 hour until loaves are firm to the touch. Turn out of pans and cool on rack.

Rose Wilder Lane in 1906

As a teenager, Rose Wilder realized that she did not share her parents' satisfaction with life in the country. She was deeply independent and ambitious to join the newly formed ranks of "bachelor girls" who were successfully invading the workforce in big cities. At seventeen, Rose was proudly self-supporting as a Western Union telegrapher in Kansas City. Her travels as a telegrapher were widespread, but she finally settled in San Francisco, where she married Gillette Lane in 1909. After a successful career as one of California's first female real estate salespersons, Rose Wilder Lane drifted into journalism. Her work for the *San Francisco Bulletin* taught her the craft she followed for the remainder of her life. By 1920, Rose was a nationally known author of fiction and nonfiction which appeared both in book form and in the popular magazines of the era. For Laura, Rose's career was an inspiration, a goal that finally expressed itself in the writing of the Little House books.

Miracle Rolls

A perfectly plain dinner roll—you can begin these a day or two ahead.

2 cups boiling water
1 tablespoon salt
⅓ cup granulated sugar, plus 1 tea-
  spoon (divided use)
⅓ cup lard

2 packages granulated yeast
¼ cup warm water
2 eggs
8 cups flour

1. Combine boiling water, salt, ⅓ cup sugar, and lard and stir until everything is dissolved. Let cool to lukewarm.

2. Dissolve yeast in warm water with remaining 1 teaspoon sugar. Let stand.

3. When sugar mixture has cooled, add eggs, yeast mixture, and 4 cups flour. Beat well. Mix in remaining flour 1 cup at a time. Refrigerate dough in plastic bag or tightly covered container. You can keep this dough for several days before using it.

4. When ready to use, preheat oven to 350°. Remove dough from refrigerator and divide in half. Form each half into sixteen round rolls. Place on a greased cookie sheet. Cover with towel and let rise until doubled in size, about 1 hour.

5. Bake for about 15 minutes or until light brown.

The Wilders' mailbox brimming with fan mail

No detail was too small for avid readers of the Little House books to overlook; Laura's voluminous mail from fans was often filled with questions about the life her books described. When a young reader wrote to inquire about the sourdough bread that sustained the Ingalls family during *The Long Winter*, Laura replied:

> Sourdough was really a substitute for sour milk and was used in cooking just as sour milk was. We had no baking powder in those days and used soda with sour milk or sour dough. To start it, Mother mixed warm water and flour, a pinch of salt and a little sugar, making it about as thick as gravy. This was kept in a warm place until it soured. It was then used as sour milk to make the biscuit, but a little of it was left to help start the next batch souring. Enough more water and flour, sugar and salt were added to make enough for use again. We used it only when we had no milk, which of course is better.

Brioche

A festive roll for a special brunch.

1 envelope granulated yeast	*1 egg*
¾ cup milk, scalded and cooled to	*2 egg yolks*
lukewarm	*½ teaspoon lemon extract*
¼ cup granulated sugar	*Small amount salad oil*
¼ teaspoon salt	*1 cup confectioners' sugar*
2½ cups flour	*2 tablespoons hot water*
⅓ cup butter, melted and cooled	*½ teaspoon vanilla*

1. Dissolve yeast in lukewarm milk in a large bowl. Add sugar, salt, and 1 cup flour and mix until smooth.

2. Beat butter into yeast mixture. Add egg and egg yolks one at a time, beating after each addition. Add remaining flour and lemon extract and beat for 5 minutes until a soft dough forms.

3. Form the dough into a ball and brush with a little salad oil. Cover with a towel and put in a warm place to rise until the dough has doubled in size, about 1½ hours.

4. Punch the dough down and divide it into thirds. Cover and let rest for 10 minutes.

5. Grease twelve muffin cups. Divide two sections of the dough into six portions each and place each portion in a muffin cup. Make a firm depression in each with your thumb. Divide remaining dough into twelve balls and press one ball into each roll. Cover and let rise until doubled in size, about 1 hour.

6. Preheat oven to 375°. Bake brioche until golden brown, about 12 minutes. Cool on rack before frosting.

7. Mix confectioners' sugar, water, and vanilla together until smooth. Frost brioche.

French Bread

*T*here is nothing in the world that smells as good as bread baking. . . .

2 packages granulated yeast
2½ cups warm water
7½–7¾ cups flour
1 tablespoon salt

1 tablespoon granulated sugar
Cornmeal
1 egg white mixed with 1 tablespoon
water

1. Dissolve yeast in warm water; let stand 5 minutes.

2. Combine 2 cups flour, salt, and sugar, either by hand or in heavy-duty mixer. Add 4½ cups flour, 1 cup at a time, to make a stiff dough. Let rest 10 to 15 minutes.

3. Turn dough out on a lightly floured surface. Knead for 15 minutes until elastic, working in ¾ to 1 cup more flour. (If you have a doughhook attachment on your mixer, you can knead the dough in the mixer instead. Knead for 10 minutes.)

4. Lightly coat a large bowl with cooking oil. Put dough in the oiled bowl, turning to grease all over. Cover and let the dough rise in a warm, draft-free place until it has doubled in size—about 1½ hours. Punch it down and let it double again—about 1 hour. Turn the risen dough out on a lightly floured surface. Divide it in half or in thirds and let it rest 10 minutes.

5. Form the dough into two large or three medium loaves by rolling each piece into a rectangle and rolling the rectangle up tightly, as if it were a jelly roll. Taper the ends and place on a greased cookie sheet which has been sprinkled with cornmeal. Depending upon the size of your cookie sheet, you may need more than one to allow space for bread to rise. Cover and let rise

until doubled once again—about 1½ hours.

6. Preheat oven to 375° and place a shallow pan of boiling water on bottom of oven. Brush the loaves with egg white glaze and cut three diagonal shallow slits on top of each loaf with a razor or a very sharp knife.

7. Bake 20 minutes and brush again with glaze. Continue to bake until the loaves are golden brown, about 30 minutes more. Loaves should have a hollow sound when tapped on bottom. Remove to rack to cool. (If you divide dough into thirds, the loaves will take less time to bake.)

The south end of the farmhouse living room

Poppy Seed Crescents

36–48 ROLLS

*T*his is a sweet roll like a brioche. If 36 rolls are too many for you to use at one time, refrigerate part of the dough and filling to use later.

1 cup milk
1 envelope granulated yeast
½ cup butter
½ cup granulated sugar, plus 3
  tablespoons (divided use)
½ teaspoon salt
1 teaspoon vanilla

4 eggs
5 cups flour
1 (13–14-ounce) can poppy seed
  filling
⅓ cup finely chopped nuts
1 egg, mixed with 1 tablespoon
  water

1. Heat ¼ cup milk in small saucepan until it begins to bubble around the edges. Cool to lukewarm.

2. Dissolve yeast in scalded milk.

3. Heat remaining ¾ cup milk in a small saucepan. Add butter, ½ cup sugar, and salt and stir until butter is melted. Cool and add vanilla.

4. Beat the eggs in a large bowl. Add yeast and milk mixtures to the beaten eggs. Beat in 2½ cups flour and then add remaining flour ½ cup at a time and knead until satiny and elastic. This can be done with a heavy-duty mixer. Cover and let the dough rise until it has doubled in size, about 1½ hours.

5. Punch down the dough and divide it into three parts. Cover and let it rest for 10 minutes. Grease three cookie sheets.

6. Shape each piece of dough into a ball. Flatten each ball gently with your hand and then roll it lightly in all directions until it forms a circle approxi-

mately ⅛ to ¼ inch thick. Spread each circle with a third of the poppy seed filling. With a pizza cutter, cut circle into twelve to sixteen wedges and roll each wedge tightly into a crescent. Place crescents on the greased cookie sheets. Cover with a dish towel and let the crescents rise until doubled in size.

7. Preheat oven to 400°. Combine remaining 3 tablespoons sugar and nuts. Brush the crescents lightly with egg wash and sprinkle with sugar-nut mixture. Bake 12 to 15 minutes until browned. Cool on racks.

The Wilders' organ

Eggs in a basket on the farmhouse porch

As farmers did, the Wilders rose early on Rocky Ridge. While Almanzo did chores in the barn, Laura prepared breakfast. The cookstove was fired up and heating while Laura made the trip to the spring to fetch the milk, cream, and butter. Before there was an electric refrigerator, the spring in the ravine kept foods cool. Then Laura cooked the first hearty meal of the day. Rose, after years of living in cities, remarked on the generous quality of the farm breakfast her mother prepared. As she described it . . . "Here are bowls of oatmeal, with whole pints of cream, large dishes of baked apples, the blue platter full of sizzling ham, with many eggs disposed upon it; here are hot cakes piled by tens and dozens, with melting butter and brown sugar between them, and hashed brown potatoes, Graham bread and white bread, fresh butter, honey, jam, milk and the steaming pot of coffee . . . Doughnuts or gingerbread accompany the coffee cups' second filling, and then—for he was a boy in New England—my father likes just one medium-size wedge of apple pie to top off the meal and finish the foundation for a good day's work."

Orange Nut Bread

1 LOAF

*T*his is delicious spread with whipped cream cheese!

2 cups flour	*1 egg, beaten*
1 teaspoon baking soda	*1 cup orange juice*
¾ teaspoon salt	*2 tablespoons lemon juice*
½ cup granulated sugar	*Grated rind of 1 orange*
¾ cup coarsely chopped pecans	*¼ cup butter, melted*

1. Preheat oven to 350°. Grease a small loaf pan and line with greased wax paper.

2. Sift together flour, baking soda, and salt. Stir in sugar and pecans.

3. Combine egg, orange juice, lemon juice, grated orange rind, and melted butter. Add dry ingredients, stirring just until mixed.

4. Pour batter into prepared pan and bake for 1 hour.

5. Remove from oven and let stand for a minute or two. Invert onto rack, remove the paper carefully, turn right side up, and allow to cool.

Laura's "Household Hints" collection

Laura, in her role as Household Editor for the *Missouri Ruralist*, was attuned to timesaving methods of housekeeping. Especially during World War I, when higher efficiency and greater productivity were encouraged on farms, Laura's minute-saving hints were shared with readers. Here is one of them: "A few days ago, I ran away from a thousand things waiting to be done and stole a little visit with a friend. And so I learned another way to cut across a corner and save work. Here it is, the way Mrs. Craig makes plum jelly: Cook the plums and strain out the juice; then to three cups of the boiling juice add four cups of sugar and stir until dissolved. Fill jelly glasses at once and set to one side. If the juice is fresh, it will be jelled in the morning; but if the juice is from canned plums, it takes longer and may have to set over until the next day. But it jells beautifully in the end."

Orange Rolls

3 DOZEN ROLLS

A delightful variation of the sticky bun!

½ cup butter	*¼ cup shortening*
2 cups granulated sugar	*2 teaspoons salt*
1 cup orange juice	*1 cup boiling water*
¼ cup grated orange rind	*¾ cup cold water*
2 packages granulated yeast	*2 eggs, slightly beaten*
½ cup warm water	*7½ cups flour*
1 tablespoon granulated sugar, plus	*¼–½ cup melted butter*
* ½ cup (divided use)*	

1. Grease 36 muffin tins. Combine butter, 2 cups sugar, orange juice, and rind in saucepan and boil for 6 minutes, stirring constantly. Spoon 1 tablespoonful glaze into each muffin cup. Set tins aside.

2. Dissolve yeast and 1 tablespoon sugar in warm water. Let stand 5 minutes.

3. Mix ½ cup sugar, shortening, salt, and boiling water until shortening melts. Add cold water.

4. Mix yeast, sugar mixture, and eggs in large bowl. Add 6½ cups flour and mix well. Turn the dough out on floured surface and knead in remaining flour. Cover with towel. Let rest for 10 minutes.

5. Divide dough into three portions. Roll each portion into a 10 x 12-inch rectangle. Brush with melted butter and roll tightly as for jelly roll. Cut each roll into twelve pieces and place one piece in each muffin cup with a cut side up. Cover and let rise until doubled in size, about 1 hour.

6. Preheat oven to 375°. Bake rolls for 15 minutes or until lightly browned. Remove from oven and let stand for 30 seconds. Shake rolls onto rack to cool.

A bowl of lemons on the farmhouse porch

Farm women have always been wage-earners and partners in their husbands' business," wrote Laura Wilder when the question of workingwomen was hotly debated during the World War I era. "It is rather amusing to read flaring headlines announcing the fact that women are at last coming into their own," she continued. "Farm women have always been business women, but no one has ever noticed it." With her customary quiet practicality, Laura slipped into a new profession when she became secretary and treasurer of the Mansfield Farm Loan Association in 1917. The loan company was a branch of the Federal Loan Bank, designed to provide low-interest loans to farmers who wished to increase or improve their land. For ten years Laura interviewed clients, completed loan applications, and doled out nearly a million dollars of government money to ambitious Ozark neighbors. Laura watched with pride as she saw her involvement with the loan company improving rural life. To her satisfaction, examiners found her work consistently accurate, and never did she issue a loan that wasn't repaid.

Lemon Spice Puffs

*T*he spice here is cinnamon sugar!

¾ cup milk, scalded and cooled
6 tablespoons granulated sugar,
*   plus 1 tablespoon (divided use)*
1 teaspoon salt
5 tablespoons butter
1 tablespoon grated lemon peel

1 teaspoon lemon juice
2 eggs, beaten
1 envelope yeast dissolved in ¼ cup
*   water*
3 cups flour
1 tablespoon cinnamon

1. Combine all ingredients except flour, cinnamon, and sugar in mixer bowl. Add the flour 1 cup at a time, beating well after each addition. Cover bowl with towel and let rise until double, about 1½ hours.

2. Grease 18 muffin cups. Combine cinnamon and sugar.

3. Punch dough so it deflates and let rest for 10 minutes. Divide dough among prepared muffin cups and sprinkle with cinnamon sugar. Cover with towel and let rise until double, about 1 hour.

4. Preheat oven to 375°. Bake puffs about 20 minutes until light brown. Turn out on rack to cool.

Rose Wilder Lane and the Wilders' 1923 Buick

From 1924 to 1936, Rose Wilder Lane made her headquarters at her parents' Rocky Ridge Farm. She made periodic trips and spent two years in Albania, but her most successful writing was accomplished on the farm, including the pioneer novel *Let the Hurricane Roar*. While Rose occupied the family farmhouse, friends constantly dropped in for visits and tea. Writing to a friend in California, Rose re-created teatime in the farm kitchen . . .

I will now take out the angel-food, or would you rather have the butter-rolls fresh this morning? or pie? I make perfectly scrumptious pies, all varieties, with crust— SUCH crust, mm! And I will make a pot of tea and we will have tea right here. The flour bin and the sugar bin . . . are window seats with hinged tops, under the north windows; and between them is the mixing cabinet with convenient zinc top . . . So you sit on the flour and I sit on the sugar and with Montgomery Ward's finest American semi-porcelain between us we'll take tea.

Raisin Tea Ring

A not-too-sweet bread for afternoon tea.

3 cups flour	¾ cup butter
7 tablespoons granulated sugar (divided use)	1 cup raisins
	1 egg
4 teaspoons baking powder	¾ cup milk, plus extra if needed
1 teaspoon salt	½ cup chopped walnuts or pecans

1. Preheat oven to 425°. Grease cookie sheet.

2. Sift flour, 6 tablespoons sugar, baking powder, and salt together in a large mixing bowl.

3. Using two knives or a pastry blender, cut in butter until mixture forms tiny balls. Stir in raisins.

4. Mix egg and milk and stir into flour mixture. If necessary, add additional milk to make a soft dough.

5. Turn dough out on cookie sheet and shape into a long roll about ¾ inch thick. Twist the roll into a ring. Sprinkle the ring with 1 tablespoon sugar and gently press in nuts. Let rest for 20 minutes.

6. Bake for 20 to 25 minutes until firm and browned. Slide onto rack to cool.

Laura's famous gingerbread cooling on the counter

Desserts

Laura Ingalls Wilder's Gingerbread

Cora's Cream Cake

Daffodil Cake

Lydia's One-Egg Cake with Chocolate Frosting

Applesauce Cake

Apple Upside-Down Cake

Charlotte de Pommes

Saucepan Cocoa Brownies

Shortbread

German Sour Cream Twists

Gingernuts

Molasses Cookies

Oatmeal Cookies

Lemon Sticks

Rose's Strawberry Pie

Apple Tart

Apple Slump

Apple Pudding

Rocky Ridge Pudding

Cup Custard

Peach Tapioca

Baked Pears

Lemon Ice Cream

Peanut Brittle

Laura Ingalls Wilder, like other celebrities, was sometimes asked to share a favored recipe. To such requests, Laura invariably supplied her gingerbread recipe, a lifelong favorite. The gingerbread became widely known when it was published in a special Laura Ingalls Wilder issue of *The Horn Book Magazine* in 1953. In the years since, Laura's gingerbread has been the feature of thousands of celebrations held in her honor all over the world. Rose Wilder Lane recalled the gingerbread well, and her own first experience in preparing it . . .

I was ambitious to make it and my most vivid memory of it is my first one. My mother was not at home; she had given me permission to make a gingerbread to celebrate something—perhaps her birthday or my father's, a family affair. I was eleven or twelve years old. I was excited of course and nervous but I made the gingerbread carefully, measuring everything, and watched its baking. My mother often left me to watch the bread baking and it seems to me now that every time she did it I was lost in a book until my mother rushed into a house full of smoke and snatched cinders of loaves out of the oven. The gingerbread, however, baked perfectly, and I had just taken it out of the oven when the minister came to call. All the duties of hostess were mine unexpectedly, and I felt important. I welcomed the minister, seated him in the "front room," spoke politely about the weather and such, then excused myself for a minute and returned with napkins, glasses of water, and three pieces of the hot gingerbread, proudly served. The minister was surprised and pleased. He looked slightly startled at first but ate a piece slowly. He declined a second and soon left. I ate none myself, saving it for the special supper that evening. I would not have cut it for anyone but such a caller as the minister. After supper, as its climax, my father, my mother, and I each took a piece of the beautiful, soft, red-brown ginger-bread, as tempting as any my mother had baked, a triumph for me. And it burned, it seemed to blister our tongues. I had used cayenne pepper by mistake, instead of ginger.

Laura Ingalls Wilder's Gingerbread

1 9-INCH SQUARE LOAF

*T*his was one of Laura's favorite recipes. There is nothing quite like the aroma of gingerbread baking. Serve this warm or at room temperature. It is delicious with applesauce or with cream that has been whipped to soft peaks and sweetened just a little.

1 cup brown sugar
½ cup shortening
1 cup molasses
2 teaspoons baking soda
1 cup boiling water, measured in a
*   2-cup (or larger) measuring*
*   cup*

3 cups all-purpose flour
1 teaspoon each ginger, cinnamon,
*   allspice, nutmeg, and ground*
*   cloves*
½ teaspoon salt

1. Preheat oven to 350°. Grease a 9 x 9-inch baking pan.

2. Blend the sugar and the shortening and mix in the molasses.

3. Add the baking soda to the boiling water and mix well.

4. Combine the flour and the spices and sift. Combine the sugar-molasses mixture with the flour mixture and the baking soda-water liquid. Mix ingredients well and pour into prepared pan.

5. Bake for 45 minutes or until cake tester inserted in the center of the gingerbread comes out clean.

A pitcher of cream on the kitchen counter

Desserts were few and far between during Laura's childhood on the prairie. Sugar was expensive, white flour often hard to get, and fruit was usually unavailable except for dried apples. In *On the Banks of Plum Creek*, Ma's simple vanity cakes provided a treat for a country party, but when Laura was asked for a recipe she admitted that she could not be specific. "I know they were mostly egg and fried in deep fat as doughnuts are," she replied. "They were to be eaten hot. Were crunchy, not sweetened and were so light . . . that they seemed to melt in one's mouth." As an adult living in the heart of the fruit-growing country, Laura prepared abundant desserts, from cobblers, pies, and cakes, to pudding and cookies. Her afternoon teas always included a sweet, whether the Wilders were alone or with company. One unexpected visitor recalled how Laura quickly prepared a simple graham-cracker sandwich while the teakettle boiled. She mixed confectioners' sugar into thick cream to make a frosting to spread between the layers of crackers.

Cora's Cream Cake

1 tablespoon butter
1 cup granulated sugar
1½ cups flour
2 heaping teaspoons baking powder
Pinch salt

1 egg
1 cup milk
1 teaspoon vanilla
Whipped Cream Frosting (see
recipe below)

1. Preheat oven to 350°. Grease two 8-inch cake pans; line with greased wax paper.

2. Cream butter and sugar in medium bowl.

3. Mix together flour, baking powder, and salt, and stir into sugar mixture.

4. Combine egg, milk, and vanilla and beat into batter. Pour batter into prepared pans and bake for 30 minutes until cake tester inserted in center of cake comes out clean. Let cool 10 minutes; take out of pans and remove wax paper. Cool on rack.

5. Fill and frost cake with whipped cream frosting.

Whipped Cream Frosting

1 cup cold heavy cream
2 tablespoons confectioners' sugar

½ teaspoon vanilla

Combine all ingredients in bowl and beat until stiff.

Daffodil Cake

1 10-INCH ROUND CAKE

*I*f you make this cake during daffodil season, arrange a few flowers in a glass of water in the center of the cake!

1 cup flour
1½ cups granulated sugar (divided use)
1¼ cups egg whites (10–12), at room temperature
¼ teaspoon salt

1¼ teaspoons cream of tartar
½ teaspoon vanilla
4 egg yolks
½ teaspoon grated lemon rind
Lemon Frosting (see recipe on facing page)

1. Preheat oven to 375°.

2. Sift flour and ½ cup sugar together.

3. Combine egg whites and salt; beat until foamy. Add cream of tartar and beat to soft peaks. Gradually beat in remaining 1 cup sugar until egg whites are stiff.

4. Fold the flour-sugar mixture into the egg whites, adding the vanilla.

5. In a separate bowl, beat egg yolks with the lemon rind until thick and light. Fold half the egg white mixture into the egg yolks.

6. Spoon batters alternately into 10-inch tube pan and bake 30 to 35 minutes. Invert pan until cake has cooled. Remove cake and frost.

Lemon Frosting

Grated rind and juice of 2 lemons (6–8 tablespoons juice)
½ cup butter

1 (1–pound) box confectioners' sugar

1. Beat together the lemon rind, juice, and butter.

2. Add sugar gradually, beating until spreadable.

Laura's rocking chair on the farmhouse porch

Lydia's One-Egg Cake
with Chocolate Frosting

1 8-INCH LAYER CAKE

*T*his is a basic, one-bowl cake dressed up with a special frosting! If you want to skip the chocolate frosting, bake the cake in a tube pan and sprinkle the batter generously with cinnamon sugar before you bake it.

1 cup granulated sugar
⅓ cup butter
1 egg
2 cups cake flour
2½ teaspoons baking powder

¼ teaspoon salt
1 teaspoon vanilla
⅔ cup milk
Chocolate Frosting (see recipe on
*   facing page)*

1. Preheat oven to 375°. Grease and flour two 8-inch cake pans.

2. Cream sugar and butter. Beat in egg.

3. Sift together flour, baking powder, and salt. Mix vanilla into milk.

4. Add flour and milk mixtures to sugar mixture alternately three times, beating after each addition.

5. Pour batter into prepared pans and bake for 20 minutes or until firm in center. Remove from oven and let stand for 2 minutes then turn out on rack to cool.

6. When cool, frost with chocolate frosting.

Chocolate Frosting

3 squares unsweetened chocolate
2 tablespoons butter
2½ tablespoons cornstarch
⅓ cup milk
1½ cups confectioners' sugar

2 egg yolks
Pinch salt
1 teaspoon vanilla
Small amount of heavy cream,
    if needed

1. In top of double boiler, over simmering water, melt chocolate with butter.

2. Blend cornstarch with milk until smooth and stir into chocolate, stirring constantly until smooth and thickened.

3. Mix 1 cup sugar, egg yolks, and salt. Add to chocolate mixture; cook, stirring, until smooth. Add vanilla; remove from heat and allow to cool.

4. Beat in remaining sugar, adding a little heavy cream if necessary to make frosting easier to spread.

When World War II food rationing started in 1942, all American kitchens, including the one on Rocky Ridge Farm, were affected. The Wilders used their government-issued ration books like everyone else, and Laura figured out carefully what groceries she could buy. As farmers, the Wilders grew most of the vegetables and fruits they ate, but items like meat and sugar were often scarce. A heartfelt surprise was enclosed in a letter from one of Laura's fans in 1944: a sugar stamp. "Perhaps your sugar allotment is not sufficient to permit you to make Mr. Wilder gingerbread or a pie as often as you would like to," the letter writer explained. Wartime recipes abounded to ease shortages and Laura collected them, including Lydia's One-Egg Cake. Lydia may have been Lydia Morgan of Danbury, Connecticut, a friend of Rose's who was entertained on Rocky Ridge. The wartime scrimping was not a significant hardship for Laura; all her life she had made the most from the simplest resources.

Laura Ingalls and Almanzo Wilder in 1943

As Laura became more heavily involved in the writing of her books in the late 1930s and early 1940s, her formal entertaining dwindled to rare occasions. One of them was Almanzo's eighty-third birthday in February 1940. For this event, guests once again filled the Rocky Ridge farmhouse. Although Almanzo was usually quiet and reserved, he enjoyed a gathering of old friends and could become witty and animated and full of stories. Though retired from active farming for many years before his death at ninety-two in 1949, Almanzo was constantly busy around the house, the barn, and the garden. He loved his goat herd and was proud of the milk production. Almanzo kept close records on the goats and was happy to report to the *Mansfield Mirror* that "Spot has given her own weight in milk every eight days since the first day of April." The Wilders drank the goat milk and Laura made butter and cheese from the pans of cream Almanzo brought in from the barn.

Applesauce Cake

*Y*ou can add a cup of raisins or chopped nuts to this cake if you like.

½ cup butter
1 cup granulated sugar
1 egg
1¾ cups flour
½ teaspoon salt

1 teaspoon cinnamon
½ teaspoon ground cloves
1 teaspoon baking soda
1 cup applesauce

1. Preheat oven to 350°. Butter and flour 9-inch tube pan.

2. Cream butter and sugar. Beat in egg.

3. Sift flour with spices. Mix baking soda into applesauce. Add these alternately to butter-sugar mixture and stir until combined. If you are adding raisins or nuts, mix them into the sifted flour and spices before combining with the butter-sugar mixture.

4. Turn into tube pan and bake 40 to 50 minutes.

5. Remove cake from pan and cool on rack.

Apples in a basket on the farmhouse porch steps

With the purchase of Rocky Ridge came hundreds of apple trees, bundled and waiting for a home in the ground. A glance at his farmland convinced Almanzo that his wheat-raising days were ended; the land was more suited to dairying and orcharding. While the apple trees sat in burlap, Laura and Almanzo worked to clear planting space for them. Together they removed brush and felled trees. Laura pulled one end of the crosscut saw and through the first year on Rocky Ridge, she was Almanzo's most frequent helper. When the trees were planted, Almanzo used simple organic farming methods. He fertilized with wood ash and manure. He allowed no hunting on his land, so the quail were thick in the orchard, eating insects that otherwise could have harmed the trees. In seven years, the trees came into bearing. The Missouri Pippins and Ben Davis apples were finely flavored and free of flaws. Production reached carload shipments to big cities, and the apples were also marketed around Mansfield. The Wilders took such a personal interest in their orchard that they could discuss the individual trees. If Almanzo mentioned "the tree that leans to the north," Laura knew exactly which one he meant.

Apple Upside-Down Cake

1 8-INCH SQUARE CAKE

*T*ry this with juicy peaches, too.

¼ *cup brown sugar*	1 *cup flour*
2 *teaspoons cinnamon*	2 *teaspoons baking powder*
2–4 *apples, depending on size*	½ *cup cooking oil*
(about 3 cups of slices)	½ *teaspoon salt*
2 *tablespoons butter*	1 *teaspoon vanilla*
3 *eggs*	

1. Preheat oven to 350°. Generously butter 8-inch cake pan.

2. Sprinkle brown sugar and cinnamon over bottom of pan.

3. Peel and slice apples and arrange over sugar to cover bottom of pan. Dot with butter.

4. Beat eggs until light in color. Mix flour and baking powder and stir into eggs with the oil, salt, and vanilla. Pour batter over apples and bake for 45 minutes until firm and lightly browned.

5. Invert pan on heatproof platter and gently shake out cake. Serve hot with whipped cream, slightly sweetened and with a little cinnamon added.

The rock house

When Rose Wilder Lane returned to Mansfield in 1928 after an Albanian sojourn, she fulfilled a long-held plan: to assist her parents and move them to a modern home. After thirty-five years of hard work, Laura and Almanzo were ready to retire from farming. Most of their land was quiet pasture and meadow. On an acreage across the ridge from their white farmhouse was a gentle ridge shaded by oaks and walnut trees. On that site Rose's dream took shape: an English-style rock cottage. The proceeds from Rose's popular Ozark short stories built the place for her parents. In its quiet setting the rock house was compact and picturesque. During construction Rose and Almanzo stood sentinel, supervising the workmen. Rose loved house-building and was meticulous in her judgments and adamant in her directives. News that the famous Rose Lane was building a house spread through the Ozarks. The curious came to gape and admire. Before the Wilders moved in, their new home was already a sensation. On Christmas Eve, 1928, Rose turned the keys over to her mother. Laura and Almanzo lived in the rock house for eight years before returning to the original house on Rocky Ridge.

Charlotte de Pommes

A thrifty, homey dish of simple, readily available ingredients, the classic recipe for this is made with buttered bread. Serve warm with ice cream or slightly sweetened whipped cream.

8–10 tart apples, peeled, cored, and quartered
2 cups granulated sugar
1 cup water
2 teaspoons vanilla

3 tablespoons butter, plus butter for pan
1 sponge cake
6 ounces currant jelly

1. Preheat oven to 325°.

2. Simmer the apples in the water with the sugar until the water is almost evaporated. Add the vanilla and the butter and continue to simmer, stirring carefully to keep some chunks of apple intact, until the mixture holds together somewhat, another 3 to 4 minutes.

3. Butter an 8-cup charlotte pan or other straight-sided pan.

4. Line the bottom and sides of pan with slices of sponge cake. Invert a juice glass in the center of the pan and pack the stewed apples around it. Remove the glass and spoon the currant jelly into the cavity.

5. Bake the charlotte for 1 hour. Remove from oven and allow to rest for 10 minutes. Invert pan on a heatproof dish and gently shake the charlotte out.

The kitchen at Rocky Ridge farmhouse

When Laura and Almanzo Wilder were settled in the rock house, Rose remodeled the original family home. It had become a place of rural beauty and comfort. "The house is the sort you would want a person named Rose Wilder Lane to live in," wrote a reporter who visited from the *Kansas City Star*. Rose herself described the kitchen, one of her favorite rooms . . .

Your car comes up the short but steep climb from the highway and stops in circle that goes around the iris bed under the elms. You confront a well all but buried in . . . honeysuckles; an expanse of cracked cement; and the screened back porch. It's a narrow porch, so almost at once you're in the kitchen, which was once a ramshackle woodshed and still hasn't a straight corner or an inch of level flooring in it. However it's at first glance quite gayly amusing. The ceiling is wood, enameled ivory and so shiny that it reflects all below it as in water; it especially reflects the walls covered with oilcloth in a bold and flaunting pattern of huge red flowers . . . Luckily there's not much of this; the walls are mostly cabinets and windows. They are all painted a lovely sunshine-yellow, with white panels . . . The range, in a recess, is Skelgas, in gray and white porcelain with black lines, and the refrigerator, electric, Westinghouse, also recessed so that its front looks even with the wall. The wavy floor is covered with linoleum . . . curtains, "gold" marquisette. There are narrow shelves over the two north windows . . . and on these stand an array of domestic animals in china—the hen that came full of mustard years ago, the cow that contained bath-salts . . . quite worthless, but amusing.

Saucepan Cocoa Brownies

*T*hese chocolate delights are a perfect project for a rainy afternoon.

½ cup butter
6 tablespoons unsweetened cocoa
1 cup granulated sugar
½ teaspoon vanilla

2 large eggs
¾ cup flour
¼ teaspoon salt
1 cup coarsely chopped nuts

1. Grease 8 x 8-inch pan and line with wax paper. Preheat oven to 325°.

2. Combine butter and cocoa in medium saucepan. Heat over low heat, stirring, until shortening is melted. Set aside to cool.

3. When cocoa is lukewarm, beat in sugar and vanilla. Beat in eggs, one at a time. Add the flour and salt and beat just until combined. Stir in nuts.

4. Pour into prepared pan and bake for 25 minutes or until top is dull. Turn out on rack; remove wax paper, and cut into squares.

A letter from Ma Ingalls resting on the farmhouse porch swing

W aste not, want not" . . . "Never complain of what you have" . . . "Where there's a will, there's a way" . . . those were principles that Laura Ingalls Wilder heard from her mother throughout her growing-up years. The platitudes Caroline Ingalls preached were practiced through necessity; she typified the frontier woman who created homes through thrift, ingenuity, and improvisation. During a decade of covered-wagon moves, Ma Ingalls kept house in unfinished claim shanties, a railroad camp, a dugout, and in isolated cabins in the woods and on the prairies. In 1887, the Ingalls family finally settled into their final home on Third Street in De Smet, Dakota Territory. It was the journey's end, a place where Ma could keep house and move no more. When she was widowed in 1902, Ma managed to support herself and her blind daughter, Mary, with the same quiet courage she had lived by all her life. And as her three other daughters married, she continued to be their adviser and counselor. "Mother's advice does help," said Laura, "and lessons learned at mother's knee last through life." Laura continued to learn from Ma, even after she was a capable housewife on Rocky Ridge Farm. Letters often passed between them, with Ma offering her wise counsel, right up to the time of her death in 1924. In the pictured letter, Ma offers suggestions for the use of grapes, a cash crop on Rocky Ridge Farm in 1913.

—98—

Shortbread

*L*ess rich than usual, this shortbread can also be used as a tart pastry.

½ cup butter
6 tablespoons granulated sugar
1 egg yolk

2 cups flour
3 tablespoons milk

1. Combine butter, sugar, and egg yolk in food processor. Add flour and milk alternately four times. Form pastry into ball; wrap and chill at least ½ hour.

2. Preheat oven to 375°. Roll dough out on a cookie sheet—or press out with fingers—into a rectangle about 5 x 10 inches.

3. Prick all over with a fork and bake 20 minutes. Shortbread should be firm but not browned. Cut into squares while hot.

Laura's quilt and sewing box

German Sour Cream Twists

*T*his dough keeps in the refrigerator for about three days.

3½ cups flour
1 teaspoon salt
2 teaspoons granulated sugar, plus
  1 cup (divided use)
1 cup shortening, at least ½ butter

1 package dry yeast dissolved in
  ¼ cup warm water
¾ cup sour cream
1 whole egg, plus 2 egg yolks, beaten
1 teaspoon vanilla

1. Preheat oven to 350°

2. Sift flour, salt, and 2 teaspoons sugar into mixing bowl. Cut in shortening.

3. Mix dissolved yeast with sour cream, eggs, and vanilla. Stir in flour mixture.

4. Form dough into flattened ball; wrap in plastic wrap, and refrigerate for at least 1 hour.

5. Divide dough into thirds and return two thirds to refrigerator. Working quickly, sprinkle some sugar on a pastry cloth or other rolling surface. Roll dough into a 6 x 9-inch rectangle. Sprinkle lightly with more sugar and fold into thirds. Repeat rolling, sugaring, and folding two more times using about ⅓ cup sugar for each third of dough. Refrigerate. Repeat with remaining two portions of dough. Refrigerate all dough when you are not working with it.

6. Roll out again and cut into strips ½ x 3 inches. Transfer strips to a cookie sheet, twisting them once or twice. You will need one *ungreased* cookie sheet for each portion of dough. You can also form them into a horseshoe shape.

7. Bake for about 20 to 25 minutes until brown. Cool on rack.

Laura's hat, gloves, and parasol

By the time she was fifty, Laura Wilder was a notable character in the little mountain community of Mansfield. The *Missouri Ruralist* profiled Laura in a feature titled "Let's Visit Mrs. Wilder" and cited her success as a businesswoman, a farm wife, a club woman, and a rural activist. But perhaps the tribute Laura appreciated most was from one of her neighbors. "Mrs. Wilder," it was said, "is a woman of delightful personality, and a combination of energy and determination." She was also Mansfield's most stylish egg lady. When she delivered eggs in town, she came complete with gloves, hat, and a parasol to shield herself from the hot Missouri sun. "Oh yes," said an old neighbor, "Mrs. Wilder was just *it*!" "We were in awe of her," said another. "People in those days just didn't make trips to California and St. Louis the way she did." When she came to town, Laura was the personification of dignity. "She always walked *so* straight," recalled a townsman. Another described her perhaps the most accurately: "Mrs. Wilder was a *gentlewoman*, much in the way that we might speak of a *gentleman*."

Gingernuts

*T*hese are a comfort cookie!

½ cup butter
1 cup granulated sugar, plus extra
  for rolling
1 egg, beaten

2 cups flour
¼ teaspoon each ground cloves and
  cinnamon
1 tablespoon heavy cream

1. Preheat oven to 350°. Grease cookie sheet.

2. Cream butter and 1 cup sugar. Beat in egg.

3. Sift flour with spices and beat into sugar mixture with cream. Mixture will be quite stiff.

4. Form into walnut-sized balls, roll in remaining granulated sugar, and place on cookie sheet.

5. Bake 15 minutes or until firm to the touch.

Laura Ingalls Wilder and schoolchildren

In schoolrooms around America, children were engrossed by Laura's account of pioneer life in the Little House books. They wrote her letters by the thousands, telling of their enjoyment of her stories and their own experiences in preparing pioneer food, drawing scenes from their favorite books and creating miniature log cabins and dugouts. Wrote one Iowa teacher: "The children have really lived with you in Wisconsin, in Indian Territory, on Plum Creek and in Dakota Territory. They call you Laura, just as if you were their nearest and dearest friend." The children of Mansfield, Missouri, had the opportunity of knowing the author of the Little House books personally. They knew her white farmhouse along the highway, and saw her downtown, at church, or at the library. Imagine the excitement in 1950 when the fourth-grade class of the Mansfield school was invited to a tea party—given by Laura Ingalls Wilder! Mansfield school children participated in the dedication of the town library named in Laura's honor in 1951, an event that pleased her greatly. And to celebrate her eighty-seventh birthday in 1954, she visited the local elementary school, where the cafeteria prepared one of her favorite meals, chicken and dumplings.

Molasses Cookies

ABOUT 4 DOZEN COOKIES

*T*hese are a hearty, old-fashioned cookie jar cookie!

⅓ cup butter
⅓ cup granulated sugar
1 egg
½ cup molasses
1 cup flour
½ teaspoon allspice
¼ teaspoon nutmeg
¼ teaspoon ground cloves

½ teaspoon salt
¼ teaspoon baking soda
1 teaspoon baking powder
1½ cups rolled oats (not instant)
1 cup grated or flaked coconut
1 teaspoon orange extract or grated
*   orange rind*

1. Preheat oven to 325°. Grease cookie sheets. You will need four cookie sheets, or you can bake cookies in two batches.

2. Cream butter and sugar. Beat in egg and then molasses.

3. Stir together dry ingredients and add to shortening mixture along with orange extract.

4. Drop by tablespoonfuls on cookie sheets and bake 15 to 18 minutes. Cookies are done when an impression made by lightly touching the center does not remain.

5. Remove from pan and cool on rack.

The cookie jar in the Rocky Ridge farmhouse kitchen

A ll of the work of a farm centers in the farmer's wife's kitchen," Laura observed. There she churned butter, skimmed milk, packed eggs, and prepared bran mash for chickens and potato parings for hogs. She also cooked for hired men, preserved fruits and vegetables, and did the weekly baking. Laura considered the kitchen her workplace, her role as a farmer's wife her occupation. Laura was so comfortable with the life she led as a farm woman that she had no qualms entertaining unexpected callers while carrying on her work. Once she would have hustled company into the parlor. But eventually, with her characteristic good sense, she remarked that "Friendliness not genuine in a kitchen is not improved by a parlor." Callers often settled down to visit with Laura at the kitchen table to discuss the local news and what was happening in the world. Her wit, her life of wide experience, and her pleasure derived from other people made Laura a memorable hostess.

Oatmeal Cookies

*B*ake half of these cookies now and form the remaining dough into a sausage shape. Wrap it in plastic wrap and freeze it. When you are ready for more cookies just slice and bake.

2 cups flour
1 teaspoon baking powder
1 teaspoon each cinnamon and nutmeg
4 cups rolled oats (not instant)
1 cup raisins
1 cup chopped nuts

2 cups brown sugar
½ cup each lard and butter, melted and cooled
2 large eggs
½ teaspoon baking soda dissolved in 4 tablespoons hot water

1. Preheat oven to 325°. Grease cookie sheets. Plan on fitting twelve cookies on each cookie sheet.

2. Sift flour with baking powder and spices. Stir in oats, raisins, and nuts.

3. Cream sugar with lard and butter. Beat in eggs, one at a time.

4. Add flour mixture and hot water mixture to sugar mixture and beat until just combined.

5. Drop tablespoons of dough on cookie sheets and bake 16 to 18 minutes until cookies are firm to touch. Remove from pan and cool on a rack.

The Wilders' table

While she was completing the writing of *These Happy Golden Years* in 1942, Laura received a request from The Scribbler's Club of Topeka, Kansas, to visit her on Rocky Ridge Farm. "I have never lost my timidity with perfect strangers," Laura admitted, but nonetheless she welcomed the group of writers who traveled 350 miles to meet her and Almanzo. Laura showed the visitors through her unique home, pausing in the library, her writing den, and Rose's twelve-windowed upstairs sleeping porch where *Let the Hurricane Roar* was written. Laura told the story of her own beginnings as a writer and answered questions from the group. When asked what her favorite books were, Laura laughed and replied that "People I wouldn't associate with I don't want to see in a book!" The summer afternoon visit concluded with a ritual Laura was familiar with from years of club meetings: tea and refreshments served in the dining room.

Lemon Sticks

*T*hese look very fragile but hold up well. People really like them so they won't last long.

½ cup butter
1 cup confectioners' sugar (divided use)
2 eggs, separated

1 cup flour
2 teaspoons grated lemon rind
1 tablespoon lemon juice
½ cup chopped walnuts

1. Preheat oven to 350°. Grease 9 x 13-inch pan.

2. Cream butter and ½ cup sugar. Beat in egg yolks one at a time, until batter is light yellow in color.

3. Mix in flour and lemon rind. With fingers, press dough into prepared pan.

4. Bake for 10 minutes and remove from oven. Cookies will be firm but not brown.

5. While dough is baking, make meringue by beating egg whites to soft peaks. Still beating, gradually add remaining ½ cup sugar and lemon juice.

6. Sprinkle nuts over dough and spread meringue over all. Bake 20 to 25 minutes longer until meringue begins to brown.

7. Cool and cut into 3 x 1-inch strips.

Rose's Strawberry Pie

1 10-INCH PIE

It is the most marvelous strawberry dish you ever tasted; far better than strawberry shortcake. I always stand the berries points up, and use big ones. The runty little ones make the syrup.

—Rose Wilder Lane

Baked 10-inch piecrust (see recipe for Hot Water Piecrust on facing page)
3 pints strawberries

½ cup water
1 cup sugar
3 tablespoons cornstarch
Whipped cream, sweetened slightly

1. Sort 1 pint of the smaller or imperfect berries and cook in water, boiling for 3 or 4 minutes. Mix sugar with cornstarch and add to glaze, stirring constantly, until glaze is clear and thick, about 3 minutes. Set aside to cool slightly.

2. Arrange remaining berries in pie shell. Pour lukewarm syrup over, coating every berry.

3. Chill and serve with whipped cream.

Hot Water Piecrust

1 10-INCH CRUST OR TOP
AND BOTTOM CRUST FOR SMALL PIE

½ cup shortening
¼ cup boiling water
1½ cups flour

Scant teaspoon salt
Scant teaspoon baking powder

1. Put shortening in bowl and pour boiling water over it. Stir until smooth and creamy.

2. Sift flour with salt and baking powder. Stir flour into liquid until it forms a ball. Chill at least ½ hour.

3. Roll out dough and fit into 10-inch pie plate. Prick all over with a fork and bake at 500° for 6 to 8 minutes until light brown.

Laura's baking utensils in the Rocky Ridge farmhouse kitchen

Once during the 1920s, one of Laura's pies provided her with food for thought. As she dished out pie to Rose and a visiting writer friend from New York City, she heard her daughter remark: "I would rather have made that pie than to have written a poem." The New Yorker chimed in with his praise for Laura's baking, exclaiming, "Oh these Missouri pies; never before have I seen such wonderful pies." "It was just a plain, farm apple pie," Laura thought, "the kind we all make in Missouri." Reflecting on the making of the Rocky Ridge pie, Laura traced its origins to the orchard she helped plant and tend, the kitchen she had designed, and the years of homemaking skills she had perfected. "Thinking of pies and poems," she declared, "I am more content with pie making, for surely it is better to make a good pie than a poor poem."

Apple Tart

1 10-INCH TART

You can cheat on this one and buy frozen puff pastry! Or you can make your own a day or two ahead and refrigerate.

4 apples, peeled, cored, and sliced	Easy Puff Paste (see recipe on
½ cup water	facing page
½ cup butter, in small pieces	6 egg yolks
Grated rind and juice of 2 lemons	1½ cups sugar
(6–8 tablespoons)	

1. Combine apples and water in medium saucepan, cover and simmer a few minutes until apples are tender and water is almost gone. Stir in butter, lemon rind, and juice. Set aside.

2. Preheat oven to 400°. Line 10-inch tart pan or pie plate with puff paste crimping edges high to hold filling. Refrigerate until ready to fill.

3. Beat egg yolks until light in color; beat in sugar. Stir in apples and pour into crust.

4. Bake 23 to 25 minutes or until filling is set and lightly browned. Cool on rack. Filling will firm up more as it cools.

Easy Puff Paste

ABOUT 2 POUNDS PASTRY,
ENOUGH FOR 2 TARTS

1. Sift flour and cream of tartar. Cut butter and shortening into ½-inch pieces

2 cups flour, plus more for rolling   *½ cup cold butter*
   out if needed   *½ cup cold shortening*
½ teaspoon cream of tartar   *⅔ cup water*

and drop into flour. Mix lightly.

2. Add all but 2 tablespoons water, folding it in from edge of bowl with spatula. Add remaining 2 tablespoons water if necessary to get dough to form a ball. Turn out onto floured pastry cloth or board.

3. Working quickly and with light strokes, roll dough into a rectangle about ⅛ inch thick. Fold bottom up and top down over that. Wrap in plastic wrap and refrigerate at least ½ hour. Roll out into a rectangle ½ inch thick and repeat the folding; refrigerate again. Repeat the rolling and folding 2 more times. You may need to flour the dough lightly to prevent sticking. Chill overnight.

4. Dough is ready to use. Roll ¼ to ⅛ inch thick for tart.

Apples on the ground at Rocky Ridge Farm

In the Missouri Ozarks, colorful explanations of the rugged countryside abounded. Of the topography, one Ozarker explained: "Our mountains ain't so high but our valleys sure are deep." Laura grew deeply interested in the history of her adopted homeland. She wrote: "The Ozarks are not really mountains, they are valleys. The Ozark streams have cut such deep valleys that the land between them is steep, high mountains. So the skyline is always level and blue like the sea, and nearly always there is a lovely blue haze over all the hillsides cut so deeply into this old, old land."

Apple Slump

*T*his is a very filling dessert.

*6 large apples, peeled, cored, and
quartered*
*¾ cup granulated sugar (divided
use)*
1 teaspoon allspice
½ teaspoon nutmeg
*1 cup water with 1 teaspoon
vanilla added*

2 cups flour
3 teaspoons baking powder
½ teaspoon baking soda
1 teaspoon salt
4 teaspoons butter
1½ cups buttermilk

1. Preheat oven to 325°. Butter 2-quart ovenproof casserole.

2. Put apples in casserole. Combine ½ cup sugar and spices and sprinkle over apples. Pour vanilla water over apples.

3. Make biscuit dough: Combine flour, remaining sugar, baking powder, baking soda, and salt. Cut in butter. Mix in buttermilk until just combined.

4. Pat dough into shape to fit top of casserole dish and put over top of apples. Cover lightly with foil.

5. Bake 30 minutes; remove foil. Bake 30 to 40 minutes longer until biscuit is baked and golden brown. Serve warm.

A single apple on the farmhouse porch

The farm is grand, really," Rose declared when inviting a New York editor to visit Rocky Ridge. "Quite cool and remote and covered by big trees. We have a good Middle Western cook and Simmons beds and saddle horses and dogs, and we'll take you on an Ozark fox hunt . . . And by the fireplace on evenings I can tell you such true stories of the people here as never can be printed. We'd love to have you drop in . . ." Rose reveled in the quiet Rocky Ridge surroundings while she wrote, but she also relished company and stimulating discussions. Friends from afar came visiting regularly during the 1920s and 1930s. Literary friends from both coasts stopped mid-continent to enjoy Rocky Ridge hospitality. Visitors from Hungary, England, and Switzerland arrived. Artists, editors, novelists, and actors came to stay. Groups of visiting newspaper staff members from nearby Springfield were invited for informal writing seminars with Rose. Mansfield acquaintances regularly called on Rose for chess games, waffle breakfasts, picnics around the fireplace, and parties on the roof garden over the garage. Rose's friend, nurse and writer Helen Boylston, loved Rocky Ridge so much that she stayed on four years. "Those were good years," she recalled, "and we had fun!"

Apple Pudding

A custardy apple pie—delicious! Try the Hot Water Piecrust recipe from Rose's Strawberry Pie—or you can use a refrigerated store-bought crust, of course!

1 9-inch piecrust, baked in a 450°
*   oven for 5 minutes and cooled*
6 apples, peeled, cored and stewed
*   in a little water until very soft*
3 tablespoons butter
1 cup granulated sugar, plus 3
*   tablespoons (divided use)*

1 tablespoon flour
3 eggs, separated
½ cup light cream
1 teaspoon vanilla

1. Preheat oven to 350°.

2. Combine apples with the butter, 1 cup sugar, and flour.

3. Beat egg yolks with cream and vanilla; add to apple mixture.

4. Pour filling into piecrust and bake for 30 minutes until set and golden. Remove from oven and increase oven temperature to 450°.

5. Beat whites of eggs to stiff meringue, gradually adding remaining 3 tablespoons of sugar. Spread over pie and return to hot oven for a few minutes, watching carefully, just until meringue starts to brown nicely. Remove from oven, cool to room temperature, and chill before serving.

The farmhouse porch swing

During World War II, Rose Wilder Lane stoutly refused to accept a food ration card. Her decision was a matter of principle; as Rose wrote in her 1942 book *The Discovery of Freedom*: "Freedom means self-control, no more, no less." She regarded a government ration card as a license to live and she chose not to be dependent on a bureaucrat's permission to buy food. To avoid rationing, Rose raised and canned enough produce on the acreage surrounding her Danbury, Connecticut, home to feed herself through the war years. Chicken and pork were raised on a nearby farm for Rose to process and preserve. By 1943, Rose had canned 397 quarts, 453 pints, and 175 glass jars. The following year she produced 300 quarts, 243 half-pints, and 33 glass jars. In recipes calling for sugar, unrationed honey was used. Rose saw nothing unusual in her method of avoiding red tape and regimentation. "What is so unusual about women doing their own gardening and canning?" she asked one reporter who called to see how her experiment was faring. "Women have been doing this for generations," Rose added.

Rocky Ridge Pudding

*T*he apples make a wonderful difference in this Early American dish.

⅓ cup cornmeal	*¼ teaspoon ginger*
2 cups scalded milk	*1 teaspoon cinnamon*
½ cup molasses	*2 well-beaten eggs*
1 teaspoon salt	*3 apples, peeled, cored, and sliced*
¼ cup granulated sugar	*2 cups cold milk*

1. Butter a 2-quart ovenproof casserole.

2. Place the cornmeal in the top of a double boiler over gently boiling water. Pour the scalded milk over, stir. Cook, covered, for 20 minutes. Remove from heat and stir in the molasses, the sugar, and the seasonings. Beat in eggs vigorously.

3. Preheat the oven to 350°. Arrange the apples in the bottom of the casserole. Add the cooked mixture and top with the cold milk.

4. Bake for 3 hours. Milk will be absorbed and pudding will be browned. Serve warm or cold. Ice cream or whipped cream add a festive touch to this dish.

Early editions of the Little House books

In her sixties, with farmwork dwindling and leisure time a new commodity in Laura's life, she discovered a new career. For years, her daughter Rose encouraged her to write an autobiography. Laura realized not only that her frontier childhood had been unique, her experiences had, by the 1930s, become a part of the remote past. She decided to record her recollections in stories for children. "I wanted children now to understand what is behind the things they see," Laura explained, "what it is that made America as they know it." Laura's stories emerged in her first book, *Little House in the Big Woods*, published in 1932 when she was sixty-five. *Farmer Boy*, published the next year, was Almanzo's story. For the next decade, Laura's life was taken up with the creation of the Little House books, a nine-volume chronicle of her life as the daughter of a pioneer family. The other titles included *Little House on the Prairie, On the Banks of Plum Creek, By the Shores of Silver Lake, The Long Winter, Little Town on the Prairie, These Happy Golden Years*, and *The First Four Years* (all published by HarperCollins). Laura's books, which quickly became American classics, were written in a simple way, in pencil, on five-cent lined tablets that she picked up at the grocery store. She wrote, she said, "between washing dishes and getting dinner or just anytime I could."

—120—

Cup Custard

A real comfort food. You can even float a little syrup on top if you want.

For one	*For four*
1 egg	*4 eggs*
1⅓ tablespoons granulated sugar	*⅓ cup granulated sugar*
Pinch salt	*¼ teaspoon salt*
¾ cup milk	*3 cups milk*
⅛ teaspoon vanilla	*½ teaspoon vanilla*
Freshly grated nutmeg	*Freshly grated nutmeg*

1. Preheat oven to 350°. Beat egg(s), beat in sugar and salt. Stir in milk and vanilla.

2. Pour into custard cup(s). Top each with a sprinkle of nutmeg.

3. Place filled custard cup(s) in a pan of boiling water in oven for 45 to 55 minutes or until center of custard is firm. Chill.

Michael, the current house cat living at Rocky Ridge Farm

During the farming years, Rocky Ridge was a menagerie of animals. The Wilders named and doted on their farmyard livestock and the pets who wandered between house and barn. A placid Jersey cow was affectionately called Mary Ellen; goats were known as Nanko and Judy. A Morgan stallion was proudly dubbed "The Governor of Orleans." Horses were always the Wilders' special interest. They never lost their homesickness for horse and buggy days when the automobile reached the Ozark hills. One of Laura's sorrows was the necessary sale of a pony she had gentled in order to pay taxes. Dogs were treated as members of the family, from Fido, the stray adopted in 1894, to Inky, a fluffy poodle, Ring, who fetched and carried written messages, and Nero, the beloved Airedale who learned to bring the cows home. Jack the bulldog had been Laura's first pet and a bulldog named Ben was her last. After Almanzo's death, Ben was a special comfort to her. Even in her last days on Rocky Ridge, Laura befriended the wildlife on the farm. Turtles from the ravine learned to line up at the kitchen door on a regular basis. On schedule, Laura appeared with their meal of bread and milk.

Peach Tapioca

*E*veryone loves tapioca. Adding peaches gives this old favorite extra flavor.

1 egg, separated
3 tablespoons quick-cooking tapioca
6 tablespoons granulated sugar
2 cups milk

1 teaspoon vanilla
2 very ripe peaches, peeled, pitted,
   and diced fine

1. Beat egg white in small bowl with electric mixer until foamy. Gradually beat in half the sugar. The egg white should form soft peaks.

2. In medium saucepan, combine tapioca, remaining sugar, milk, and egg yolk. Cook over medium heat for a few minutes, stirring constantly, until mixture comes to full boil.

3. Pour hot mixture slowly over egg white. Stir just to blend. Stir in vanilla.

4. Allow to cool for about 20 minutes. Stir in peaches. Refrigerate until cold before serving.

Baked Pears

*C*hoose large sweet pears for this dish.

4–6 pears	*½ cup granulated sugar*
1 cup boiling water	*Freshly grated nutmeg*

1. Preheat oven to 325°. Wash pears and stand up in an ovenproof dish—a 1½- or 2-quart soufflé dish is good for this. Pears should be very near or even touching each other for support. Pour in water; sprinkle sugar over pears, and grate a dusting of nutmeg over each.

2. Cover dish—use foil if the dish does not have a cover—and bake for 1 hour. Test for tenderness with a skewer. Cool to room temperature and then chill.

3. Serve cold with slightly whipped cream or ice cream.

A bowl of pears on the kitchen table in the farmhouse kitchen

Lemon Ice Cream

*T*his is a refreshing confection. Garnish each serving with a sprig of fresh mint.

1 cup granulated sugar
3 tablespoons lemon juice

2 teaspoons grated lemon rind
2 cups light cream

1. Combine sugar, lemon juice, and rind in a medium mixing bowl. Add light cream and beat until well mixed.

2. Pour mixture in an ice cube tray or other freezerproof dish and freeze for 3 hours or until firm. Does not need to be stirred.

Lemons in a bowl on the front porch of Rocky Ridge farmhouse

The Wilders' table set with Willoware china

As a hardworking farm woman and later as an author, Laura Ingalls Wilder indulged herself only occasionally with material possessions. One rare excess was the wide variety and number of dishes that filled the kitchen and dining room cupboards. There were plenty of dishes to entertain large numbers and there were many choices and styles to select. The Wilders were especially proud of the delicate pink French Limoges Haviland china set given to them by their then-grown daughter, Rose. Another gift from Rose was the set of pink everyday dishware presented to Almanzo for Christmas in 1931. But the Wilders loved best their set of deep blue Allerton Willoware. Like many homemakers in middle America in the 1930s, Laura collected the thin, transparent dishes known as "Depression glass." Often given away free as premiums in grocery stores or in boxes of oatmeal, "Depression glass" was given scant respect. Laura collected sets in amber, pink, and green. Today, displays of the Wilder dishes at Rocky Ridge Farm reflect the ways Laura set her table through all sixty-four years of her married life.

Peanut Brittle

*T*his treat is best made on a dry day.

2 cups shelled peanuts   *1 cup water*
2 cups granulated sugar   *1 cup vinegar*

1. Butter a jelly roll pan and spread peanuts out evenly in a single layer.

2. Boil sugar and water until mixture forms thin threads when poured out of a spoon, about 10 minutes.

3. Add vinegar and continue boiling until liquid begins to turn amber in color. This takes another 7 or 8 minutes and *must* be watched carefully as mixture can easily burn.

4. Remove from heat and pour evenly over nuts, tilting pan to cover entirely.

5. Allow to stand in a cool dry place. When cooled and hardened break into pieces.

A pitcher of lemonade on the steps of the Rocky Ridge farmhouse side porch

Drinks and Snacks

Iced Coffee for Fifty

Spiced Tea

Spiced Apple Cider

Hot Chocolate

The Perfection of Lemonade

Amber Nectar

Grape Punch

Cheese Savories

Ham and Cheesies

Henny Penny Muffins

Banana Fritters

Rose's Turkish tea service

Rose Wilder Lane's world travels produced exotic tales for publication and for storytelling around the fireplace at Rocky Ridge Farm. When Rose unpacked her trunks at home she shared her souvenirs and curios with her parents and friends. "Oh, Rose!" Laura once exclaimed. "What a world!" From Albania, Rose brought a Turkish coffee set. She explained its significance . . .

It is a courtesy expected in Moslem countries that the hostess offer every caller a cup of coffee. One day I drank forty cups. The coffee is made of green beans; they are roasted over a tiny fire in the kitchen courtyard while the brass coffee pot is heated. The hot roasted beans are ground in the hot grinder, as fine as the finest flour. Three tablespoons of water are boiled in the pot—which is longhandled because it is set on the little bonfire. Three tablespoons of sugar and three tablespoons of coffee are added. The pot is snatched from the fire just before it boils over. The coffee is then poured quickly into the little cups and served. It is very sweet and rather thick, but the coffee is ground so fine that it leaves no grounds in the cup. I used to make coffee in the same way, only on the range and my mother liked it very much. She used the set after I left there.

—130—

Iced Coffee for Fifty

*Y*ou can make this really festive by topping it with whipped cream dusted with a little cinnamon sugar.

2 ½ gallons water
1 pound regular-grind coffee
Cheesecloth
½ cup cold water if needed

1 pint heavy cream, whipped
  (optional)
Cinnamon sugar (optional)

1. Bring the water to a boil in a large pot.

2. Divide the coffee among four cheesecloth bags. Use several layers of cheesecloth and tie with twine loosely to allow for swelling.

3. Place bags of coffee in boiling water. Adjust heat so the water is just simmering and cook for 10 minutes. Remove bags and allow coffee to cool. If it is cloudy, you can clear it by adding ½ cup cold water.

4. Serve in tall glasses over ice. Top with whipped cream dusted with cinnamon sugar, if desired.

The rock fireplace in the farmhouse living room

In December 1920, while Rose Wilder Lane worked as a writer for the American Red Cross in Paris, Laura planned a party for her in absentia. Logs blazed in the big rock fireplace in the parlor when guests arrived. Wherever they looked, photographs of Rose had been placed. She smiled from the mantelpiece, the library nook, from tables and ledges in each corner of the room. Everyone settled down around the fireplace with apples and nuts and cider while Laura read from Rose's letters home. She told of life in Paris, her travels in Poland, and a harrowing journey into the Albanian mountains where she was among the first foreign women seen by the highlanders. Each guest present wrote a letter to Rose, wishing her a Merry Christmas. The "Rose Party" reflected a creative mother and a unique daughter. As Laura had mused soon after Rose's birth in December of 1886: "A Rose in December was much rarer than a rose in June."

Spiced Tea

ABOUT 2 QUARTS

*F*reeze iced tea glasses before filling with the tea—it even *looks* refreshing.

1 cup granulated sugar	*2 (2-inch) sticks cinnamon*
2 cups water	*¼ teaspoon ground ginger*
Grated rind of 1 lemon	*1 quart freshly made hot tea*
8 whole cloves	*Juice of 2 lemons (6–8 tablespoons)*

1. Combine sugar, water, lemon rind, and spices in saucepan and simmer together 15 minutes.

2. Strain and add tea. Chill. Add lemon juice to taste.

3. Mix with an equal amount of water and pour over ice. For individual servings, pour ⅓ cup spiced tea into 10-ounce glass; add ⅓ cup cold water and ice to fill glass.

Spiced Apple Cider

ABOUT 1 QUART

*T*his is also delicious served warm in a mug on a frosty day!

1 quart apple cider	*1 teaspoon whole cloves*
1 teaspoon whole allspice	*1 (2-inch) stick cinnamon*

1. Combine the cider and the spices in a 1½-quart saucepan and simmer slowly for ½ hour.

2. Strain mixture and chill.

A holly tree planted by Almanzo Wilder on Rocky Ridge Farm

With their relatives far away and their grown daughter, Rose, often traveling the world as a journalist, Laura and Almanzo were sometimes alone for the holidays on Rocky Ridge Farm. But theirs was a marriage of unusually close companionship; whether in work, relaxation, or celebrating, the Wilders were contented in each other's company. At Christmastime 1920, Rose was living and working in Paris as a writer for the American Red Cross. Laura told of the quiet but happy holiday she and Almanzo spent in a letter to Laura's mother and sisters in De Smet . . .

> We were glad to get your letter . . . It came on Christmas day. Manly and I spent the day by ourselves, with roast chicken and dressing, mashed Irish potatoes, baked sweet potatoes, brown bread, white bread, blackberry jelly, doughnuts, sweet potato pie (in place of pumpkin pie), cheese and coffee for dinner. After dinner we sat by the fireplace and read and looked at our Christmas cards and letters. Then later we popped corn over the fire and ate apples and walnuts and corn . . .

Hot Chocolate

*O*n a frosty winter day, nothing warms you through and through like a steaming cup of hot chocolate. Whipping this gives it a wonderful froth—but go ahead and top it with whipped cream!

6 tablespoons unsweetened cocoa	*1 quart milk*
6 tablespoons granulated sugar	*Whipped cream*

1. Combine cocoa, sugar, and 1 cup of milk in a 1½-quart saucepan and stir to dissolve. Add remaining milk and bring to a simmer, stirring constantly. Simmer for 3 minutes.

2. Remove pot from stove and beat the cocoa with an eggbeater or a hand-held electric mixer for 2 or 3 minutes.

3. Serve in mugs with a spoonful or two of whipped cream.

Gingerbread and lemonade by the farmhouse kitchen window

During Laura's childhood, lemonade was a rare treat; on the frontier any citrus fruit was an exotic luxury. Later, with improved transportation methods and refrigeration, Laura knew lemonade as a staple of picnics and a common refreshment on hot Ozark afternoons. A visiting admirer of the Little House books recalled Laura's observation that a crew of laborers working on the road that ran past Rocky Ridge Farm must need a drink. She interrupted the visit to stir up a pitcher of lemonade in the kitchen. When she offered the icy pitcher and glasses to the grateful workingmen, she urged them to "rest a spell" under the shady trees along the road's edge.

The Perfection of Lemonade

*T*he rind makes the difference here.

3 lemons	*Approximately 1 quart boiling*
6–8 tablespoons confectioners'	*water*
sugar	*Sprigs of fresh mint (optional)*

1. Grate rind from 1 lemon and squeeze the juice from all three.

2. Put rind, juice, and confectioners' sugar in a 1-quart heatproof jug.

3. Fill jug with boiling water. Stir and let stand until cooled.

4. Serve over ice with a sprig of mint.

Rocky Ridge farmhouse

Laura's parties were memorable ones. Her St. Patrick's Day celebration included Celtic music on the phonograph, Irish stories and history, with green decorations. For an old-fashioned theme, Laura lit the parlor with candles and asked guests to arrive in clothing at least twenty years old. At another gathering, friends played pioneer games and each brought an antique to show. The rugs were rolled up in the parlor and fiddlers played for square dancing. Entertaining on the lush grounds around the farmhouse was a favored custom of Laura's. At one club social meeting, guests wore Gypsy costumes and were entertained around a campfire with fortune-telling and ghost stories and refreshments were served in a tent. "Fortunate indeed are those who are entertained at Rocky Ridge," declared a Mansfield friend of the Wilders.

Amber Nectar

6 (4-OUNCE) SERVINGS

*B*efore you juice the lemon, carefully cut off the zest of the lemon (the thin yellow outside skin) in one long piece. Curl it up in a chilled glass pitcher, pour in the amber nectar, and you have a pretty party refresher!

1 pint white grape juice   *1 cup water*
Juice of 1 lemon (3–4 tablespoons)   *Freshly grated nutmeg*

1. Combine juices and water. Grate in a little nutmeg.

2. Chill and serve over ice.

Grape Punch

ABOUT 2 QUARTS

*F*or a festive look, cut the peel off 1 orange, keeping it in one piece. Curl it up in a glass pitcher and add ice before pouring in the punch.

6 lemons   *1 quart white grape juice*
6 oranges   *½ cup granulated sugar, or to taste*

1. Squeeze juice from lemons and oranges.

2. Combine grape juice, lemon juice, orange juice, and sugar. Taste for sweetness and add sugar if needed.

3. Chill and serve.

The farmhouse living room

In 1915, Laura Wilder became a member of the study club called "The Athenians," which was organized at Hartville, twelve miles from Rocky Ridge Farm. Laura's impromptu meal served up for "Athenian" visitors showed her to be a relaxed hostess, as comfortable in the kitchen as she was in the parlor. She recalled the incident . . .

While busily at work one afternoon I heard the purr of a motor and going to the door to investigate, I was met with the smiling faces of Mr. and Mrs. Frink and Mr. and Mrs. Curtis of Hartville. They had come over to tell me of my election to membership of "The Athenians." What should be done when there is unexpected company and one is totally unprepared and besides must be at once hostess, cook and maid? During the first of that pleasant afternoon my thoughts would stray to the cook's duties. When the time came, however, it was very simple. While I made some biscuit, Mrs. Frink fried some home-cured ham and fresh eggs, Mrs. Curtis set the table. The Man of the Place opened a jar of preserves and we all had a jolly, country supper together before the Hartville people drove home. It is such a pleasure to have many friends and to have them dropping in at unexpected times . . .

Cheese Savories

*T*he unbaked pastry balls freeze well—just bake a minute or two longer right out of the freezer.

¼ pound sharp Cheddar cheese, cut in small cubes
¼ cup butter, cut in small pieces

½ cup flour
Pinch salt (optional)
Paprika

1. Cream cheese and butter in food processor. Add flour and salt and process until combined.

2. Form cheese mixture into 1-inch balls. Place on ungreased cookie sheet and refrigerate several hours (or freeze and then store in plastic bag).

3. Preheat oven to 450°. Sprinkle each savory with a little paprika. Bake 8 to 10 minutes. Serve hot.

Ham and Cheesies

*T*hese are worth the effort it takes to make them.

Ham Relish

1 cup ground baked ham
⅓ cup finely chopped celery
2 tablespoons sweet pickle relish
1 teaspoon horseradish
¼ cup mayonnaise
⅓ cup finely chopped chives
1 teaspoon Dijon mustard
½ cup grated sharp Cheddar
Small amount paprika

Biscuits

2 cups flour
1 teaspoon salt
2 teaspoons baking powder
¼ teaspoon baking soda
½ cup butter
¾ cup buttermilk

1. Combine all ingredients for ham relish except the paprika. Set aside while making biscuits.

2. Sift together the dry ingredients for biscuits. With a pastry cutter or two knives, cut in the butter until the consistency of coarse meal.

3. Stir in buttermilk until just combined and turn out on lightly floured surface.

4. Knead once or twice until dough just holds together. Do not overwork dough or it will be tough. Roll out lightly to about ⅓ inch thick.

5. Preheat oven to 425°.

6. With a biscuit cutter or juice glass, cut out circles, about 1⅓ inches in diameter.

7. Spread half the circles with ham mixture. Sprinkle with paprika.

8. Cut out the centers of the remaining circles with a small cutter or a thimble. Place the rings of dough on the ham circles and press around the edges with a fork.

9. Grease a cookie sheet and place the ham and cheesies on it. Bake for 18 minutes until lightly browned and serve hot. You'll probably have extra filling—it's good on celery or crackers!

After publishing her 1938 best-selling pioneer novel *Free Land*, Rose Wilder Lane settled permanently in a quaint farmhouse in Danbury, Connecticut. There she indulged her favorite hobbies of house renovation, needlework, and entertaining. Her brick-floored country kitchen became a gathering place for New York literati and friends from around the world who arrived for short or extended stays. Rose relished conversation over coffee cups as she explored her friends' ideas of life, literature, and politics. Two favorite guests were native Missourians, the writer Norma Lee Browning and her husband, photographer Russell Ogg. As their mentor, Rose helped lead them into successful careers. Norma Lee and Russell spent the summer of 1939 with Rose in Danbury. Rose cooked them memorable meals, and snacks of cinnamon rolls and popcorn. She also successfully taught Norma Lee the writing craft. Russell spent the summer remodeling Rose's house, and displayed a skill as an expert baker of pies. Rose shared Russell's pie-making techniques with her mother, who always remained interested in new recipes.

Apples by the farmhouse kitchen window

The Wilder home on Rocky Ridge was a house of many windows. Dozens of vari-sized windows, from cubbyholes to large sheets of clear glass, brought sunlight and pastoral scenes into the farmhouse. Curtains hung straight at the sides of the windows, leaving the views undisturbed. As Laura moved from room to room, the meadows and trees and hills outside became her living landscapes. "I don't want curtains over my pictures," Laura explained. "They're never the same for two hours together and I like to watch them changing." In the kitchen, windows flanked the wide counter where Laura mixed and kneaded bread. Every week of her married life she baked bread and she never grew to like the dusty dryness of the flour or the rhythmic movements of kneading the dough. So as she prepared bread, Laura concentrated on the views she saw from the windows: the oak trees, the duck pond, and redbirds on the lawn. "She has windows everywhere," Rose remarked. "Not only in her house but in her mind."

Henny Penny Muffins

3 DOZEN MINI MUFFINS

A savory muffin—serve with drinks or as a snack.

2 tablespoons chopped celery
2 tablespoons chopped onion
4 tablespoons butter, melted
2 cups flour
½ teaspoon salt
4 teaspoons baking powder

1 teaspoon thyme or sage or a mix-
ture of both
2 eggs, beaten
1 cup milk
1 cup diced cooked chicken

1. Preheat oven to 425°. Grease 36 mini muffin cups or line with paper muffin cups.

2. Sauté celery and onion in butter until soft.

3. Sift dry ingredients together into mixing bowl. Sprinkle with thyme.

4. Combine eggs, milk, chicken, and celery mixture. Add all at once to dry ingredients and stir until just combined.

5. Spoon into muffin tins and bake 12 to 15 minutes until golden brown.

Laura Ingalls Wilder

Laura Ingalls Wilder—pioneer, author, homemaker—lived long and well. Not long before her death at ninety, in 1957, she reflected on her life philosophies . . . "It has been many years since I beat eggs with a fork, or cleaned a kerosene lamp," she wrote. "Many things have changed since then, but the truths we learned from our parents and the principles they taught us are always true; they can never change. Great improvements have been made because every American has been free to pursue his happiness, and so long as Americans are free they will continue to make our country ever more wonderful."

Banana Fritters

*H*ave the batter ready and the oil heating—these make a popular after-school snack and are a good way to use up those overripe bananas!

1 cup flour
1 tablespoon granulated sugar
¼ teaspoon salt
1 egg, beaten until light
¼ cup milk

3 very ripe bananas, mashed
1 tablespoon lemon juice
Oil for deep frying
Confectioners' sugar or cinnamon
   sugar

1. Combine flour, sugar, and salt.

2. Beat egg into the milk and combine the two mixtures.

3. Stir in the bananas and lemon juice.

4. Heat oil to 365°. Drop batter by tablespoons into oil and fry until golden brown on all sides. Drain on paper towels and sprinkle with sugar. Serve while piping hot.

Index

Page numbers of illustrations are set in italics.
Index photographs are Laura's utensils from her Rocky Ridge kitchen.

Laura Ingalls Wilder

If the way is long
Let your heart be strong
Keep right on round the bend
Though you're tired and weary
Still journey on to your happy abode
Where all that you love
And are dreaming of
Will be there at the end of the road.
—Laura Ingalls Wilder